ST★RS
AND
STEPPING STONES

That Patchwork Place®

Marsha McCloskey

ACKNOWLEDGMENTS

My thanks to the Monday Night Bowling League, especially Carolann Palmer, Joan Hanson, Judy Pollard, Liz Thoman, Cleo Nollette, Laura Reinstatler, and Nancy J. Martin, who stitched quilts for me; and also to Genie Barnes for making a quilt and Marty Bowne for coloring up a storm. Thanks, too, to Judy Martin for the use of the Night Owl and Auntie's Favorite blocks from her *Ultimate Book of Quilt Block Patterns*.

CREDITS

Photography . . . . Carl Murray
Brent Kane
Robert Ehnat
Skip Howard Photos
Illustration and Graphics . . . . Stephanie Benson
Text and Cover Design . . . . Judy Petry
Editor . . . . Liz McGehee

Stars and Stepping Stones ©
© Marsha McCloskey
That Patchwork Place, Inc., P.O. Box 118, Bothell, WA 98041
Printed in the United States of America
96 95 94 93 92 91 90 89   6 5 4 3 2 1

Library of Congress Cataloging-in-Publication Data

McCloskey, Marsha.
    Stars and stepping stones / by Marsha McCloskey.
      p. cm.
    ISBN 0-943574-59-5:
    1. Machine quilting--Patterns. 2. Patchwork--Patterns.
  I. Title.
  TT835.M397 1989
  746.9'7--dc20

88-51649
CIP

Contents

Introduction

In 1986, Nancy J. Martin and I coauthored a book of quilt patterns called *A Dozen Variables.* It was a design workbook that invited the quiltmaker to go beyond the twelve quilt patterns in the book, using two simple exercises to help her design original quilts. The first exercise involved combining the Variable or Sawtooth Star blocks with alternate pieced blocks to achieve new overall quilt designs. In the second exercise, different shadings were used to bring out elements in those designs that needed emphasis. It was a simple design technique; it was fun; and we loved the quilts.

Like the quilts in *A Dozen Variables,* all the quilts in *Stars and Stepping Stones* involve stars. The other design element common to the quilts in this book is rows of squares that form chains or "stepping stones" across the quilt surface. In addition to the Variable Star used in *A Dozen Variables,* two other basic stars, the Le Moyne Star and the Unknown Star, have been included in this collection of designs.

As I looked through my quilt design books for more ideas, I came across several blocks with names like Road to Oklahoma, Railroad, and Stepping Stones — all names that lead somewhere, travel, or suggest movement. And these designs do move. The stars attract your attention, and the stepping stones lead you on and give motion to the quilt surface.

I have had fun with this group of designs. My normal method of quilt design is to make a small sketch and then go to fabric to evolve the total quilt design. But I drew the Stars and Stepping Stones designs all at once. They spilled out of my head and I had no time to make them right away. Excited about the designs, I showed them to a few friends who offered to help make the quilts. The line drawings and a few shading ideas were all I had to give them for guidance, so I asked them to just "do their own thing" with the colors, and we would see what came out.

You can see the quilts in the Gallery section, beginning on page 29. I feel very lucky to be able to include several versions of the Stars and Stepping Stones quilts, my own and those of my friends. I thank them for sharing their time and creativity so enthusiastically to help with this project.

Simple Stars

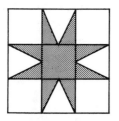

Unknown Star

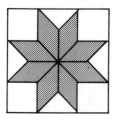

Le Moyne Star

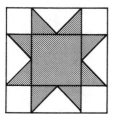

Sawtooth Star

Stars and Stepping Stones Designs

A quick survey of quilt pattern books yielded the star design blocks you see on page 6. They have both stars and rows of squares, placing them in the category of Stars and Stepping Stones designs. Also shown are some "stepping stones": alternate blocks and pieced set units that can successfully link star blocks and continue the rows of squares or chains over the entire surface of the quilt. Combining these two elements, star blocks and Stepping Stone blocks, and then coloring to emphasize the connections is what makes the characteristic Stars and Stepping Stones pattern.

Many of the Stars and Stepping Stones quilt designs are combinations of well-known patterns. In Irish Beauty (page 42), Cranberry Relish (page 44), and The Great Unknown (page 48), pieced stars are paired with Single or Double Irish Chains. Starlight Surrounded (page 52), combines the simple Sawtooth Star with the traditional Burgoyne Surrounded.

In Star Matrix (page 40) and Fifty-four-Forty or Fight (page 50), set squares of the same scale as squares within the star block serve to continue the chains through the stars across the quilt surface. Stars and Stepping Stones (page 38) is an alternate block design that evolved directly from design techniques described in *A Dozen Variables*.

Stepping Stones

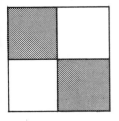

Four Patch

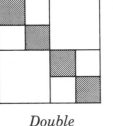

Double Four Patch

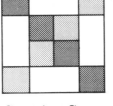

Stepping Stone

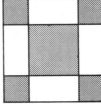

Puss in the Corner

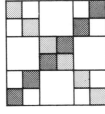

Chimneys and Cornerstones

Ninepatch

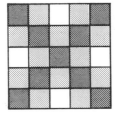

Double Ninepatch

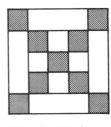

Double Irish Chain

King's Highway

Crisscross

Single Irish Chain

6

Stars with Stepping Stones

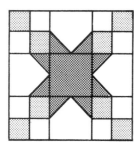

Stairway to the Stars

Stepping Stones II

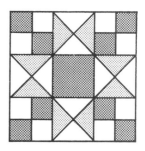

Ohio Trails

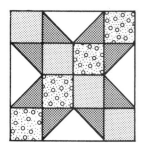

Indian Star

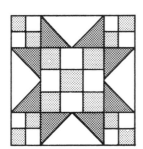

Mrs. Lloyd's Favorite

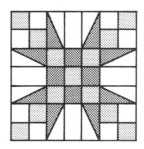

Night Owl

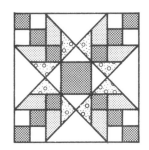

Auntie's Favorite

Arrow Points

Blackford's Beauty

Stepping Stones I

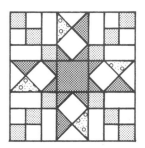

Arrowheads

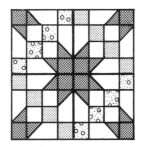

Road to California

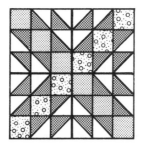

Double X

Stairway to Heaven

Quilt Planning

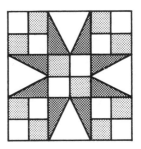

TOOLS AND SUPPLIES

Rulers: I use two rulers for drafting and drawing. Both are clear plastic with a red grid of ⅛" squares. I use a short ruler for drawing quilt designs on graph paper and a longer one, 2" wide and 18" long, for drafting designs full size and making templates.

Graph paper: Most useful is a ⅛" grid with a heavy line at the 1" increments. You can use this type for drawing quilt plans and drafting most templates. Other grids, such as ⅕" and ⅙", are sometimes needed. Most graph paper is printed in a nonreproducing blue that will not show when copied on most photocopiers.

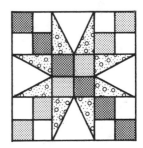

Pens: I like a fine felt-tip pen to make line drawings of quilt designs. The black lines photocopy well.

Pencils: For shading quilt drawings to determine light, medium, and dark areas of a design, a #2 lead pencil is all you really need, but a large set of colored pencils is almost as much fun as fabric.

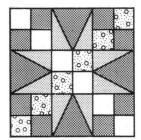

Copy Machine: I know most quilters don't own their own copy machine, but you should have access to one. I use the one at the corner grocery almost daily. Use a photocopier to make copies of line drawings, so you can shade them in several different ways before settling on the best one.

SHADING

Any patchwork design block can be shaded in several different ways. As you can see from the different shadings of the Fifty-Four-Forty or Fight star block on this page, color placement can shift emphasis from one design element to another. When blocks are set together, this potential for changing coloring is expanded to the whole quilt design. Block boundaries can be ignored for shading purposes, though they are usually maintained for ease of construction.

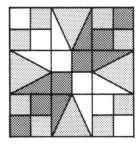

Single-square link

The illustrations on this page show the Fifty-four-Forty or Fight star block combined with three different linking blocks. When the link is a single set square the same size as the squares in the star block (left), lattices of the same scale complete the set. Shading brings out strong diagonal chains of two colors.

When the linking element is a Four Patch (below, left), lattices the width of the Four Patch complete the set. Shading is similar, but the wider lattices give the design an airier look.

In the third example (below, right), the star block is set alternately with another pieced square called Crisscross. The overall design is more complex looking, with more chains and fewer stars. The outside edge incorporates a configuration of Four Patches to create a pseudo-border; the design looked unfinished without it. Note the "circular" or curved effect created by the angle of the star points. These curves could be further emphasized with shading.

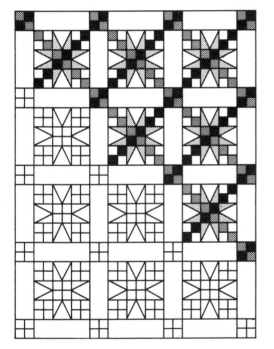

Four-Patch link

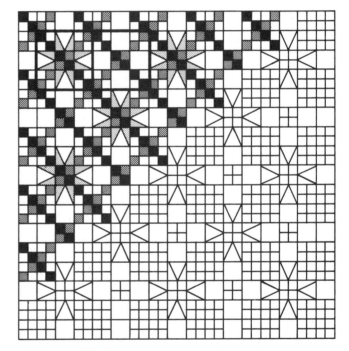

Alternate-block set

To create your own Stars and Stepping Stones design, draw a star block on 1/8" graph paper. Experiment with different shadings. Draw the block in various sets with lattice and set pieces that continue chains with the same size squares as the star block. Combine simple stars with alternate blocks like Double Four Patch or an Irish Chain block. Combine star blocks that already contain chains with single set squares, Four Patches, or Ninepatches of the same scale as squares in the block. What alternate blocks would create an interesting design? Draw your design ideas on graph paper as line drawings. Make several copies of your designs and experiment with coloring and shading.

While you are coloring, try different arrangements of light, medium, and dark tones. Keep in mind that these are relative terms. How a fabric's value is finally defined depends on the fabrics around it. Medium tones are especially changeable. They can be light when placed next to a dark fabric or dark when put next to a very light one. Sketch until you develop a light and dark relationship that seems to work. Then try it with fabric.

The stepping-stone elements in many of these designs could easily be combined with other design motifs besides stars. How about Easter Baskets Surrounded or Schoolhouse Crisscross?

When I colored the Stars and Stepping Stones line drawings, I tried to emphasize the stars and the chains of squares to go with the general theme of this book. Other quilters saw different possibilities and placed color to emphasize different design elements, sometimes obliterating the stars or stepping stones entirely.

Study the Stars and Stepping Stones quilts in the Gallery section, beginning on page 29. Several are interpretations of the same line drawings. Note the two versions of Fifty-four-Forty or Fight and also the two colorings of Irish Beauty. Starting with line drawings, the quiltmakers experimented with shading to create their own individual quilts. For each quilt in the pattern section, a line drawing is provided for you to play with. You may like my shading of the designs, or you may see other possibilities to try.

CHOOSING A DESIGN

The character of your quilt will depend on both your fabric selection and design choices. No other quilter has been where you have been, made the same choices, bought the same fabrics. Your fabric collection is unique, and your quilt will be too.

Many of the quilts presented in the Gallery are scrap or multifabric quilts. Working with many fabrics expands color and shading possibilities and makes the star blocks even more versatile.

After studying the quilts in this book, you probably will have a good idea of which quilt you want to make. The easiest way to proceed is to use an existing quilt plan. The quilt plans provided in the pattern section of this book include cutting directions, color suggestions, fabric requirements, and step-by-step instructions. If you prefer to create your own quilt designs with star blocks and stepping stones, read over the Shading section. Start your own quilt design from scratch or incorporate some of the suggestions in the Quilt Patterns, beginning on page 37.

Fabrics with good contrast

FABRIC SELECTION

To select your fabrics, begin with a color idea or theme. Though another quilt may inspire you, many times a single fabric will provide the key inspiration for color in a quilt. This main fabric or idea print will give you color clues as to what other fabrics will go with it. Think in terms of related colors and contrasts. If your idea print is dark, choose something light in a related color to go with it. When two fabrics are side by side, there should be a definite line where one stops and the other begins, to show contrast.

Contrast, both in color and visual texture, makes pieced designs more visible. Visual texture is the way a print looks—is it spotty, smooth, plain, dappled, linear, rhythmical, or swirly? Are the figures far apart or close together? Mix large prints with small prints, flowery allover designs with linear rhythmical prints. Too many similar prints can create a dull surface or one that is visually confusing. Small, regular prints will often quiet down larger, more flamboyant ones.

For best results, select lightweight, closely woven, 100% cotton fabrics. A high polyester content may make small patchwork pieces difficult to cut and sew accurately. Preshrink all fabrics before use. Wash light and dark colors separately with regular laundry detergent and warm water. If you suspect a dark color will run, rinse it separately in plain warm water until the water remains clear. Dry fabrics in the dryer and press them well before cutting.

COLOR RECIPE

Define a color recipe for your design. What color will be the dark? What the light? The recipe for Fifty-four-Forty or Fight, pictured on page 30, calls for the background to be assorted black prints and plaids; the squares that chain one way are assorted greens and the other way, assorted maroons. The star points are various grays that range from medium to very light. The inconsistency within each color group adds depth and movement to the design.

Having chosen a tentative color recipe based on your color theme and shaded sketches, select a range of fabrics for each color group in the recipe. If black is one of the colors, pick several black prints in differing intensities and visual textures. Pull every black in your collection that even remotely fits the criteria. Not all of these will be used, but it is important to study the possibilities. Do the same with each color group in the recipe.

Resist overmatching colors. As a color group, reds can range from rust to red, from maroon to brown, and still occupy the same position in the block design. A group of lights can go from a very white to ecru to medium tones. Darks can range from very dark to medium. If your color grouping looks boring, throw in a color surprise, a nonsequitur—navy in a run of browns or true red where only shades of maroon and rust have been used.

FABRIC SKETCH

Once you have chosen a Stars and Stepping Stones design, an arrangement of lights and darks, and pulled runs of fabric from your collection, the next step is to make a fabric sketch. This trial run of blocks (or block segments) will test your color recipe, the projected color arrangement.

Cut the pieces for one or more blocks from your chosen fabrics. Place the shapes on a piece of needlepunch or flannel, which has been hung on the wall, to evaluate the effect. Cut more pieces and make changes until it pleases you. When the color arrangement is set, piece the blocks. Now, cut and sew more blocks in the same recipe. Make needed color and design changes as the quilt grows. Many quilters use a reducing glass, a multiple-image Fresnel® lens, or a Polaroid® camera to view and evaluate their work.

Fabric sketch on a design wall

Feel free to experiment with different prints and color arrangements. Push yourself; be adventurous. Go beyond what you consider safe fabrics and color usage. Break a few rules. Forget about centering large motifs; cabbage roses and other large prints work better when they are cut randomly. Stripes and plaids can be cut randomly, too—even off grain, if you wish. Try using the wrong side of some prints to get just the right tone. If you make a mistake in piecing, consider leaving it in to create interest. If you run out of one fabric, substitute another and keep working.

VARYING CONTRASTS

One strategy for making quilts visually interesting is to vary the contrast in the unit blocks. High-contrast blocks are needed to establish the design, but more interest will be created when the other blocks in the quilt have lower contrast. It's okay to lose the design in some parts of the quilt. The viewer expects the same design to be regularly repeated and will search for a "disappearing" design motif.

Background fabrics are particularly important in creating variations in the contrast of the blocks. Bright whites can hold the same design spaces in blocks as ecru and more medium tones. The whites will add sparkle to the quilt and lead the eye from one part to the next. Yellow used in small amounts is, like bright white, a real eye-catcher, creating movement wherever it appears.

The coloring of the set pieces, alternate blocks, or lattices is an important part of the quilt's total look. Set pieces that are the same color as the background of the unit blocks will float the design, while those cut from contrasting fabric will outline each block and emphasize its squareness.

QUILT SIZE

The size of your quilt will depend on its intended function. You will need a quilt plan before you can buy fabric and begin sewing. A quilt plan can be a scale drawing of a quilt design on ⅛" graph paper. From such a plan, it is easy to tell the number of blocks and set pieces that will be needed to complete a given quilt, as well as finished dimensions of plain borders. Eight quilt plans for Stars and Stepping Stones quilts are provided in the pattern section. To make existing quilt plans larger or smaller, add or subtract blocks, set pieces, or borders until the desired size is reached.

Quilt Plan for Sawtooth Star and Double Four Patch
Dimensions: 40" x 52"

Cutting

Once you have decided on a design, fabrics, and a size for your quilt, it is time to cut the pieces. In quiltmaking today, we have several cutting techniques available to us. I sew all my pieced work on the sewing machine, so the way I cut my pieces is somewhat defined. The outside edges must be precisely cut so that when I sew ¼" in from that edge, my sewing line will be in the right place. No drawn sewing line is needed. For years, I have used paper pattern pieces instead of stiffened templates and cut with good-quality, sharp scissors. More recently, I have begun using a rotary cutter and ruler to cut pieces. I feel both methods have their place in my quiltmaking and I sometimes combine them if it seems the best way.

In the sections that follow, I will explain how to cut with scissors and templates and how to cut with a rotary cutter and ruler. It is up to you, the quiltmaker, to choose the cutting and sewing methods that seem the most reasonable for your project, your resources, and your skills.

Cutting with Scissors

TOOLS AND SUPPLIES

Scissors: You will need scissors for cutting paper and a good-quality, sharp pair for cutting fabric only. If your fabric scissors are dull, have them sharpened. If they are nearly "dead," invest in a new pair; it's worth it.

Template Material: To make templates, you will need graph paper or tracing paper, removable drafting tape, lightweight posterboard (manila file folders are good) or plastic, and a glue stick.

Markers: Most marking of cutting lines on fabric can be done with a regular #2 lead pencil and a white dressmaker's pencil. Ask at a fabric or quilt shop about the different kinds of marking pens available. Whatever you choose, first test it on your fabric to make sure the lines won't bleed.

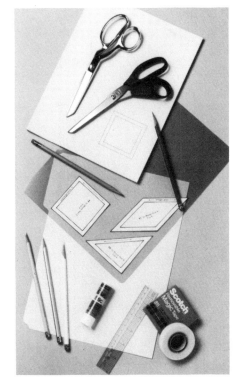

TEMPLATES

The templates beginning on page 55 are multi-use templates intended to fill the needs of as many quiltmakers as possible. If you cut with scissors, you will need a set of pattern pieces or templates to make each unit block design.

Carefully trace the templates from the book onto graph

Using a paper template

Making a stiffened template

paper or tracing paper. Trace accurately and transfer to the paper all information printed on the templates.

Use templates as paper patterns to cut around with scissors or in conjunction with a ruler and rotary cutter. Use stiffened templates to trace around before you cut. Paper templates are simply cut out and used. To make stiffened templates, roughly cut out the pattern pieces outside the cutting line. Glue each one to a thin piece of plastic (X-ray film is good) or lightweight posterboard. Cut out the paper pattern and its stiffening together. Be precise. Make a template for each shape in the design.

Study the design and templates. Determine the number of pieces of each shape and each fabric to cut. Trim the selvage from the fabric before you begin cutting. When one fabric is to be used both for borders and the unit block designs, cut the borders first; then cut the smaller pieces from what is left (see Borders on page 62).

At the ironing board, press and fold the fabric so that one, two, or four layers can be cut at one time. Fold the fabric so that each piece will be cut on the straight grain. Linear prints, such as stripes and checks, should be cut one at a time if you want the design to line up with seam lines.

When using a stiffened template, position it on the fabric so the arrows match the straight grain of the fabric. With a sharp pencil (white for dark fabrics, lead for light ones), trace around the template on the fabric. This is the cutting line. Cut just inside this line to most accurately duplicate the template.

For a paper template, line it up with the straight grain of fabric. Hold it in place on the fabric and cut around it. Be precise. Compare cut pieces with the template to be sure they are true. Paper templates can also be used to help guide your rotary cutting when odd shapes are needed. With removable tape, tape the template to the bottom of a clear plastic guide or position the template on the fabric and carefully place a ruler on top of it to provide a straight edge for the rotary cutter. Be careful not to slice off bits of the template as you work. In machine piecing, there are no drawn lines to guide your sewing. The seam line is ¼" from the cut edge of the fabric, so the outside edge must be precisely cut to ensure accurate sewing.

Always make one sample block of a design before embarking on a large project. After cutting the necessary number of pieces of each color and shape for one unit block, arrange the pieces on a flat surface in the desired design. This will help you to determine which pieces to sew together first and to evaluate your fabric choices and arrangement.

Cutting with the Rotary Cutter

Scissors have been with us for centuries, but the rotary cutter was introduced to the quilt world in the early 1980s. It is a great tool, but with it came the need for cutting mats; special thick plastic rulers in various shapes, sizes, and markings; and plenty of refill blades.

Besides requiring a number of accessories, the rotary cutter has also changed the way quilters think about the pieces of fabric they cut. With most rotary cutting, there is no marking of either cutting or sewing lines according to a template. Careful attention must be paid to measuring each dimension before making a cut. The dimensions of the cut pieces must include proper ¼" seam allowances, and grain lines must fall in the right places.

TOOLS AND SUPPLIES

Rotary Cutter: These generally come in two sizes. I use the larger one with the 2" diameter blade. The blades are very sharp when new, so take care not to cut yourself. They are easily nicked and dulled with use, so keep a fresh refill blade on hand to avoid dull-blade frustration.

Cutting Mat: Made of various plastic materials, these mats come in several sizes and serve to protect your table and keep cutting blades sharp. My favorite mat measures 24" x 36" and covers half of my work table. A smaller 9" x 24" mat is great for taking to workshops.

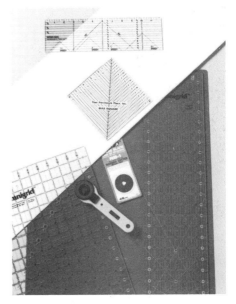

Rulers: Cutting guides for rotary cutting are ⅛" thick transparent Plexiglass™ and come in an amazing array of sizes and markings. Of all the rulers I own, these four are the ones I use the most:

1. A 6" x 24" ruler for cutting long strips. It is marked in 1", ¼", and ⅛" increments (that's important!), with both 45- and 60-degree angle lines.
2. A 15" square for cutting large squares. It is marked in 1", ¼", and ⅛" increments and is extremely useful for cutting quilt set pieces.
3. A 3" x 12" ruler. This one is handy for shorter cuts and medium-sized pieces, where the previous two rulers prove too cumbersome.
4. Bias Square™. This handy 6" square is marked in ⅛" increments with a 45-degree angle line running diagonally corner to corner. Originally invented for rotary cutting pieced half-square triangle units like those used for Sawtooth borders, this tool can be used for cutting small squares and triangles and trimming points for easy matching.

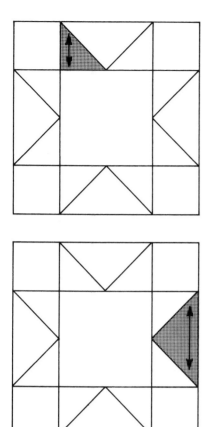

GRAIN LINES

Thread is woven together to form fabric. It stretches or remains stable, depending on the grain line that you are using. Lengthwise grain runs parallel to the selvage and has very little stretch. Crosswise grain runs from selvage to selvage and has some "give" to it. All other grains are considered bias. True bias is a grain line that runs at a 45-degree angle to the lengthwise and crosswise grains.

If fabric is badly off grain, pull diagonally in the opposite direction to straighten. It is impossible to rotary cut fabrics exactly on the straight grain of fabric, and many fabrics are printed off grain. In rotary cutting, straight, even cuts are made as close to the grain as possible. A slight variation from the grain will not alter your project.

In most cases, the rotary cutting directions include the following guides for grain-line placement:

1. Squares and rectangles are cut on the lengthwise and crosswise grain of fabric.
2. Half-square triangles are cut with the short sides on the straight grain and the long side on the bias.
3. Quarter-square triangles have the short sides on the bias and the long side on the straight grain. They are generally used along the outside edges of blocks so the long edge will not stretch.
4. The grain lines of other shapes used in this book are shown on the templates, which begin on page 55. The guiding principle is that straight grain should fall on the outer edge of pieced units and blocks.
5. When you are working with striped fabric or special prints, the direction of the stripe or print will take precedence over the direction of the grain. Handle these pieces carefully, since they are not cut on grain and will be less stable. If these pieces are to be used along the outside edges of the quilt, stay-stitch ⅛" from raw edge to avoid stretching.

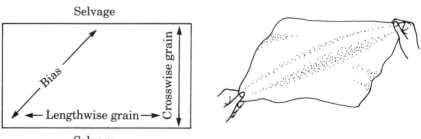

STRAIGHT CUTS

All pieces are cut with the ¼" seam allowance included. If you can sew accurate ¼" seams by machine, there is no need to mark stitching lines. To cut squares, rectangles, and triangles, you will first need to cut straight strips of fabric.

1. Align the Bias Square™ with the fold of fabric and place a cutting guide to the left. When making all cuts, fabric should be placed to your right. **Note:** Reverse these techniques if you are left-handed.
2. Remove the Bias Square™ and make rotary cut along right side of ruler. Hold ruler down with left hand, placing smallest finger off the ruler. This serves as an anchor and keeps ruler from moving. Move hand along ruler as you make the cut, making sure the markings remain accurate. Use a firm, even pressure as you cut. Begin rolling the cutter before you reach the fabric edge and continue across the fabric. Always roll cutter away from you; never pull rotary cutter toward yourself. The blade is necessarily very sharp, so be careful!
3. Fold fabric again so that you will be cutting four layers at a time. (This means shorter cuts.) Open and check the fabric periodically to make sure you are making straight cuts. If fabric strips are not straight, use Bias Square™ and cutting guide to realign.

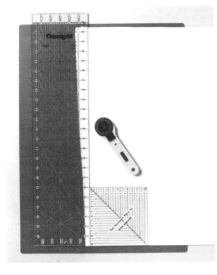
Match selvages

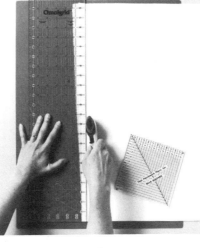
Make first cut

Four layers

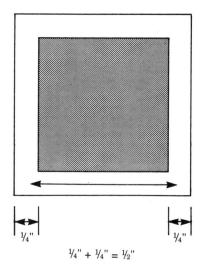

$\frac{1}{4}"$ $\frac{1}{4}"$

$\frac{1}{4}" + \frac{1}{4}" = \frac{1}{2}"$

SQUARES AND RECTANGLES

1. First cut fabric into strips the measurement of the square, plus seam allowances.
2. Using the Bias Square™, align top and bottom edge of strip and cut fabric into squares the width of the strip.
3. Cut rectangles in the same manner, first cutting into strips the length of the rectangle.

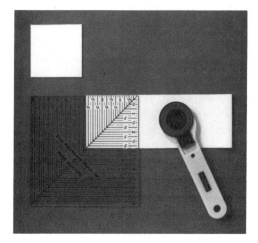

Occasionally, you may need to cut a small odd-size square or rectangle for which there is no marking on your cutting guide. Make an accurate paper template (including ¼" seam allowance) and tape it to the bottom of the Bias Square™. You will then have the correct alignment for cutting strips or squares.

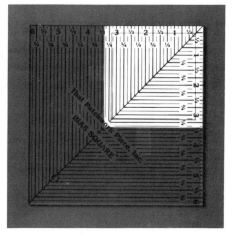

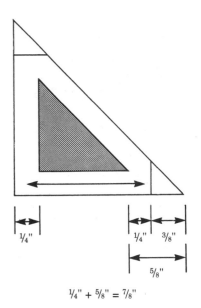

$$\frac{1}{4}" + \frac{5}{8}" = \frac{7}{8}"$$

TRIANGLES

Half-Square Triangles. These triangles are half of a square cut diagonally, with the short sides on the straight grain of fabric and the long side on the bias. To cut these triangles, cut a square and then cut it in half diagonally. Cut the square $\frac{7}{8}"$ larger than the finished short side of the triangle to allow for all seam allowances. Rotary cutting dimensions are given with each template in the Template section and in the directions for each quilt.

1. Cut a strip the finished measurement of the short side of the triangle, plus $\frac{7}{8}"$.
2. Cut into squares using the same measurement.
3. Take a stack of squares and cut diagonally corner to corner. Check the first triangles you cut against the proper pattern pieces in the Template section to make sure they are the right size.
4. Use a template or a Bias Square™ to trim points for easy matching.

Trimming Points on Half-Square Triangles for Easy Matching

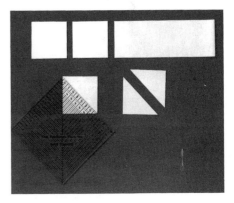

The Bias Square™ can be used to trim seam allowance points on half-square triangles. The measurement to use is the finished short side of the triangle plus $\frac{1}{2}"$ ($\frac{1}{4}"$ seam allowance on each side). The example shown here is a half-square triangle with a finished dimension of 4".

1. To quick cut this triangle, cut a $4\frac{7}{8}"$ square of fabric and cut it in half once on the diagonal.

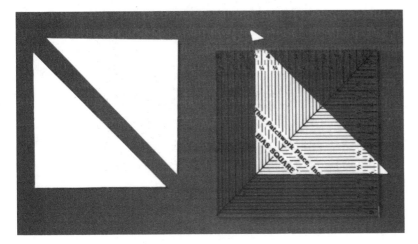

2. To trim the points for easy matching, set the Bias Square™ at the $4\frac{1}{2}"$ mark on the fabric triangle, as shown. The points of the triangle will stick out $\frac{3}{8}"$. Trim them off with the rotary cutter.

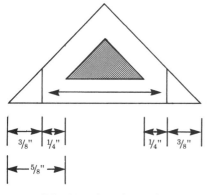

$$\frac{3}{8}" \quad \frac{1}{4}" \qquad \frac{1}{4}" \quad \frac{3}{8}"$$

$$\frac{5}{8}"$$

$$\frac{3}{8}" + \frac{1}{4}" + \frac{1}{4}" + \frac{3}{8}" = 1\frac{1}{4}"$$

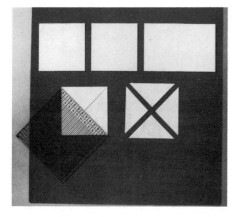

Quarter-Square Triangles. These triangles have their short sides on the bias and the long side on the straight of grain. Placing the straight grain of the triangle on the outside edges of your block or quilt keeps it from stretching. These triangles are cut from squares. The square is cut 1¼" larger than the finished long side of the triangle.

1. Cut a strip the desired finished measurement, plus 1¼".
2. Cut strip into squares using the same measurement.
3. Taking a stack of these squares, line up the ruler from corner to opposite corner and cut diagonally. Without moving the squares, cut in the other direction. Each square will yield four triangles with the long sides on straight grain.
4. Use a template or ruler to trim ⅜" points off these triangles for easy matching (see page 55).

ADDITIONAL SHAPES

Other shapes, like the triangles needed for the Unknown Star or the diamonds in the LeMoyne Star, can be cut using templates or by combining rotary and template techniques.

1. Make an accurate paper template of the desired shape.
2. For shapes with dimensions that don't match the cutting guide, tape the template to the underside to guide you as you cut the strips.
3. Subcut strips using the template as a guide.

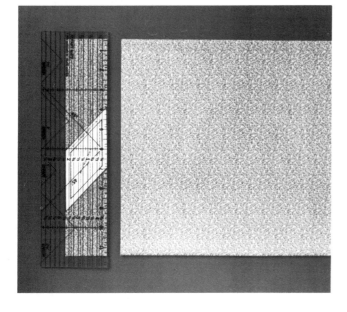

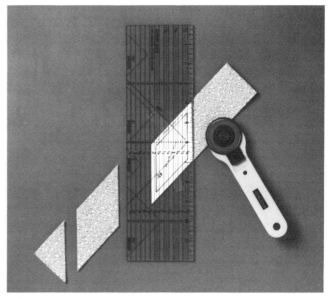

Piecing

Machine Piecing

Tools and Supplies

Sewing Machine: It needn't be fancy. All you need is an evenly locking straight-stitch. Whatever kind of sewing machine you have, get to know it and how it runs. If it needs servicing, have it done, or get out the manual and do it yourself. Replace the old needle with a new one. Often, if your machine has a zigzag stitch, it will have a throat plate with an oblong hole for the needle to pass through. You might want to replace this plate with one that has a little round hole for straight stitching. This will help eliminate problems you might have with the edges of fabrics being fed into the hole by the action of the feed dog.

Needles: You will need a supply of new sewing machine needles for light- to medium-weight cottons.

Pins: Multicolored glass or plastic-headed pins are generally longer, stronger, and easier to see and hold than regular dressmaker's pins.

Iron and Ironing Board: A shot of steam is useful.

Seam Ripper: I always keep one handy.

Scissors: A small pair is just right for clipping threads.

General Rules

For machine piecing, use white or neutral thread as light in color as the lightest fabric in the project. Use a dark neutral thread for piecing dark solids. It is easier to work with 100% cotton thread on some machines. Check your needle. If it is dull, burred, or bent, replace it with a fresh one. Sew exact ¼" seams. To determine the ¼" seam allowance on your machine, place a template under the presser foot and gently lower the needle onto the seam line. The distance from the needle to the edge of the template is ¼". Lay a piece of masking tape at the edge of the template to act as the ¼" guide. Stitch length should be set at 10–12 stitches per inch. For most of the sewing in this book, sew from cut edge to cut edge (exceptions will be noted). Backtack, if you wish, although it is usually unnecessary, as each seam will be crossed and held by another.

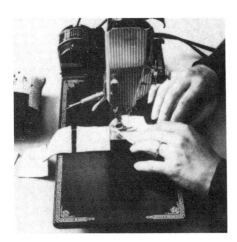

Chain piecing

Use chain piecing whenever possible to save time and thread. To chain piece, sew one seam, but do not lift the presser foot. Do not take the piece out of the sewing machine and do not cut the thread. Instead, set up the next seam to be sewn and stitch as you did the first. There will be a little twist of thread between the two pieces. Sew all the seams you can at one time in this way, then remove the "chain." Clip the threads.

In general, press the seam allowances to one side, toward the darker fabric when possible. Press seams open when indicated in piecing instruction. Avoid too much ironing as you sew because it tends to stretch biases and distort fabric shapes.

To piece a unit block, sew the smallest pieces together first to form units. Then, join smaller units to form larger ones until the block is complete.

MATCHING TIPS

These matching techniques can be helpful in making the Stars and Stepping Stones designs:

1. Opposing Seams. When stitching one seamed unit to another, press seam allowances on seams that need to match in opposite directions. The two "opposing" seams will hold each other in place and evenly distribute the bulk. Plan pressing to take advantage of opposing seams. You will find this particularly important in strip piecing.

2. Positioning Pin. A pin, carefully pushed straight through two points that need to match and pulled tight, will establish the proper point of matching. Pin the seam normally and remove the positioning pin before stitching.

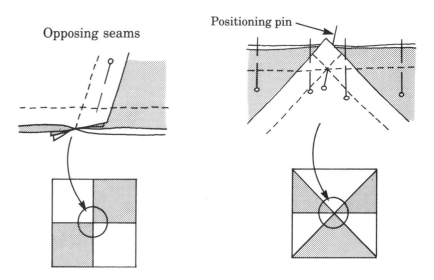

Opposing seams

Positioning pin

3. The X. When triangles are pieced, stitches will form an X at the next seam line. Stitch through the center of the X to make sure the points on the sewn triangles will not be cut off.

4. Easing. When two pieces to be sewn together are supposed to match but instead are slightly different lengths, pin the points of matching and stitch with the shorter piece on top. The feed dog will ease the fullness of the bottom piece.

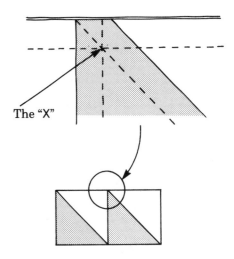

The "X"

Easing

5. Set-in Seams. Where three seam lines come together at an angle, stop all stitching at the ¼" seam line and backtack. Don't let even one stitch extend into the seam allowance. Set-in points are indicated on the design drawings by large dots. As each seam is finished, take the work out of the machine, position the next seam, and start stitching in the new direction. Backtacking is necessary because these seam lines will not be crossed and held by any other stitches.

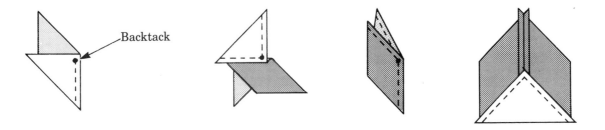

Backtack

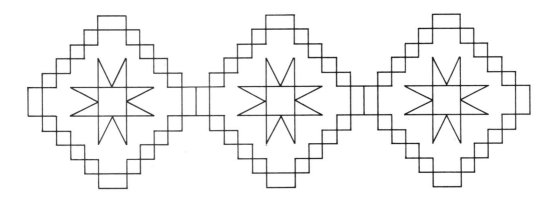

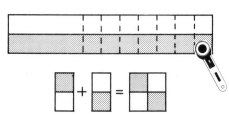

Four Patch units

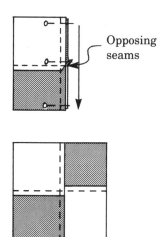

Opposing seams

Pressing

Strip Piecing

All of the patterns in this book have sections made up of squares and sometimes rectangles that make up the "stepping stone" parts of the designs. You can piece these units with the strip-piecing method described here or you can cut squares with scissors or rotary cutter and piece in the traditional manner.

Many quiltmakers feel that strip piecing is a faster way to work. Long fabric strips are sewn together in units called strata and then cut into shorter portions; the small units are then recombined to form simple designs. Strip piecing is a great time-saver when you are working with squares and rectangles that will be combined in identical colors and in repeated units.

To determine the width to cut strips, add a ¼" seam allowance to each side of the finished dimension on the desired shape. For example, if the finished dimension of a square will be 2", cut 2½" strips. Both finished and cutting dimensions are provided for squares and rectangles in the Template section that begins on page 55.

Cut strips from the length of the fabric, when possible, because it's easier to keep them on grain. When it is necessary to use the cross-grain to get the required length, be sure to straighten the fabric so strips will be cut as close to true grain as possible (see page 16). Fold the fabric so two or four layers can be cut at one time. Mark strip widths and cut with sharp scissors or use a rotary cutter and ruler. Take care and be accurate. Time saved with quick methods is wasted if the work is done poorly.

Sew long strips together with ¼" seam allowances. Press seam allowances toward the darker fabric, pressing from the top of the work so the fabric won't pleat along the seam lines. Usually, pressing toward the dark will result in opposing seams at points of matching. If the coloring of the strips doesn't work out that way, press for opposing seams instead of always to the dark.

Measure and mark crosswise cuts, using templates or rotary cutter and ruler. Join strip-pieced units, as shown in the illustrations, to make Four Patch, Ninepatch, and other desired units.

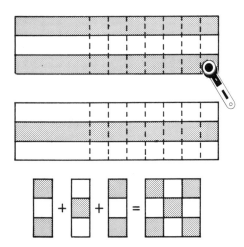

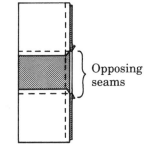

Opposing seams

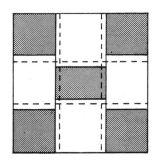

Pressing

Ninepatch units

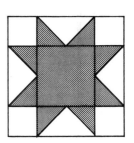

Piecing the Stars

SAWTOOTH STAR

The pretty and versatile Sawtooth Star is the simplest of the pieced star designs to make. Edge to edge, straight seam sewing makes it a snap to put together.

1. Lay the cut pieces on the table to determine which to sew together first. Starting with the triangles, piece four Flying Geese units as shown.

 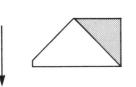 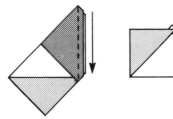

Pressing

2. Use chain piecing to sew Flying Geese units together with square patches in three rows.

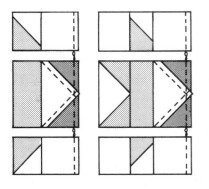 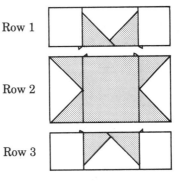

Row 1

Row 2

Row 3

3. Press to take advantage of opposing seams; then pin Row 1 and Row 2 as shown. Stitch long seam. Join Row 3 to Row 2 in the same manner. Press as shown.

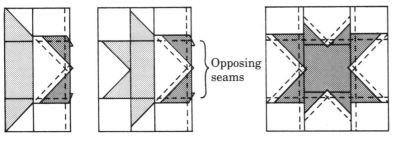

Opposing seams

Pressing

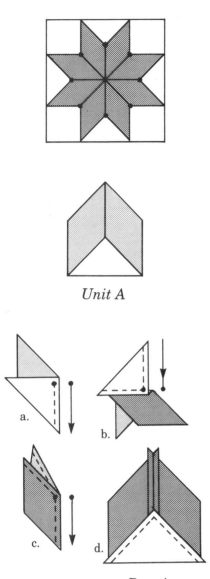

Unit A

Pressing

LE MOYNE STAR

The Le Moyne Star is one of the most basic patterns in patchwork. It has set-in seams (indicated by large dots in the illustrations) and takes a little more time to sew than Sawtooth or Unknown stars, but mastering the stitching is worth the effort.

1. Lay the cut pieces on the table to determine which to sew together first. Begin with Unit A, the diamond-diamond-triangle unit. Make four.
   a. Sew a diamond to a triangle. With triangle on top, begin to sew at the ¼" seam line. Backtack by sewing two stitches forward and two stitches back, taking care not to stitch into the seam allowance. (Backtacking is necessary here to hold the stitches as they will not be crossed and held by another line of stitching.) Sew the remainder of the seam, ending at the cut edge of the fabric. (No backtacking is necessary here as this seam will be crossed and held by another.)
   b. Sew the second diamond to the same triangle. With the triangle on top, sew from the outside edge of the fabric, ending with a backtack at the ¼" seam line.
   c. Folding the triangle out of the way, match the points of the diamonds to position them for the third seam. Stitch the diamonds together, beginning with a backtack at the inner ¼" seam line and ending at the raw edge of the fabric.
   d. With an iron, lightly press the center seam open. Press the other two seams toward the diamonds. (Sometimes, especially when working with fabric that has a low thread count, it is better to finger press while piecing to avoid stretching bias edges. Use the iron only to press the finished block.)
2. Make four Unit B. Sew a corner square to the right edge of each completed A unit. With the square on top, begin stitching with a backtack at the inner ¼" seam line and sew to the outside raw edge.

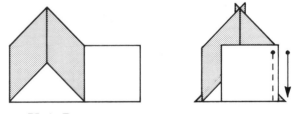

Unit B

3. Make two Unit C.
   a. Join two B units to form Unit C by first matching the corner square of one B unit to the diamond of the next. With the square on top, stitch from the outside edge, ending with a backtack at the inner ¼" seam line.
   b. To sew the diamonds together, match the points, folding the rest of the block out of the way. Use a positioning pin to match the center seams. Pin normally; remove the positioning pin. Beginning with a backtack, stitch from inner ¼"

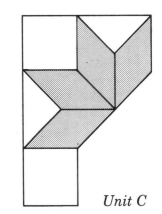

seam line through the center seams to the raw edge of the fabric. Press center seams open and corner square seams toward the center.

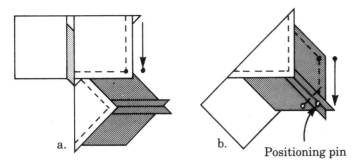

a.   b.   Positioning pin

Unit C

4. Join the C units.

a. & b. To join the two C units and complete the Le Moyne Star will take three more seams. Follow the same procedure as in step 3a to join the first two seams at the corner squares.

c. The final seam is the center seam. Use a positioning pin to carefully match the center seams at the center point. Pin the seam securely and remove the positioning pin before stitching. Backtacking at the ¼" seam line, stitch precisely through the center, ending with another backtack at the ¼" seam line.

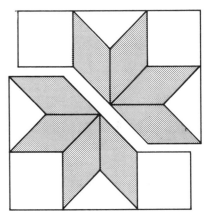

Two C units

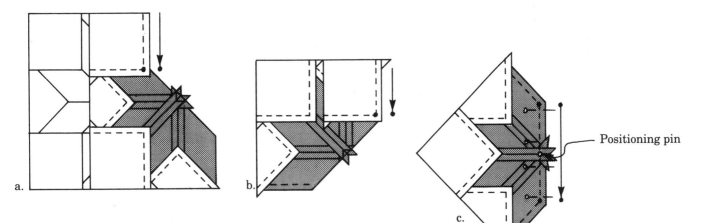

a.   b.   c.   Positioning pin

d. Press the center seam open and the remaining seams toward the center.

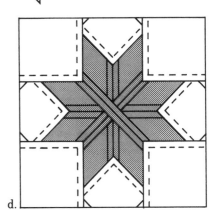

d.

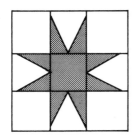

UNKNOWN STAR

The piecing of the Unknown Star is similar to the Sawtooth Star in sequence, but a little more tricky, because the skinny triangle star points are cut as mirror images and tend to be a little stretchy. The angle of the star points can give a curved look to the overall quilt designs. Look for "big circles" in quilts that feature this block.

1. Lay the cut patches on the table to determine which pieces to sew together first. Begin by stitching the four three-triangle units, as shown. Notice that the points of the long skinny triangles are cut off for easy matching and that they must be cut as mirror images (four one way, four reversed).

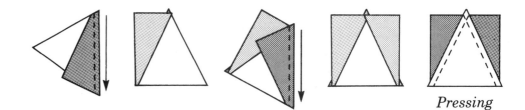

Pressing

2. Use chain piecing to sew the pieced side units together, with the square patches in three rows.

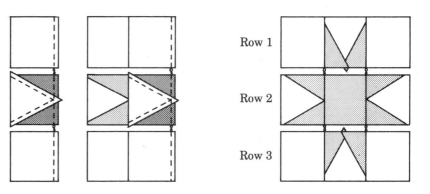

Row 1

Row 2

Row 3

3. Press to take advantage of opposing seams; then pin Row 1 and Row 2 together, as shown, and stitch the long seam. Join Row 3 to Row 2 in the same manner. Press as shown.

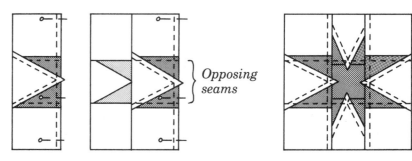

} *Opposing seams*

Pressing

Gallery

Irish Beauty by Liz Thoman, 1988, Bellevue, Washington, 41" x 55". In this alternate coloring of the quilt pattern given on page 42, each pastel Le Moyne Star is framed by rows of squares of the same color.

Irish Beauty by Marsha McCloskey, 1989, Seattle, Washington, 42" x 56". This small quilt combines two traditional quilt designs, the Le Moyne Star and Double Irish Chain, and then sets them on point. Quilted by Virginia Lauth.

Stairway to Heaven by Marsha McCloskey, 1989, Seattle, Washington, 22" x 22". Borders added to a design block that was left over from another quilt create this sunny wall hanging.

Fifty-four-Forty or Fight by Marsha McCloskey, 1986, Seattle, Washington, 45" x 53". Lattices and cornerstones the same scale as squares in the star block continue the stepping stones diagonally across the quilt. A sprinkling of white with variations in contrast of the many fabrics gives this quilt considerable sparkle. Quilted by Freda Smith.

Fifty-four-Forty or Fight, Quilters Anonymous Raffle Quilt, 1989, Edmonds, Washington, 91" x 105". A Chain-of-Squares border frames this version of Fifty-four-Forty or Fight. The stars seem to dance on the light background, suspended by the chains of squares.

The Great Unknown by Nancy J. Martin, 1988, Woodinville, Washington, 51" x 63 1/2". Careful handling of color in the outside Irish Chain blocks creates a pieced-border effect, as the Unknown Star blocks form big circles in the quilt design. Quilted by Virginia Lauth.

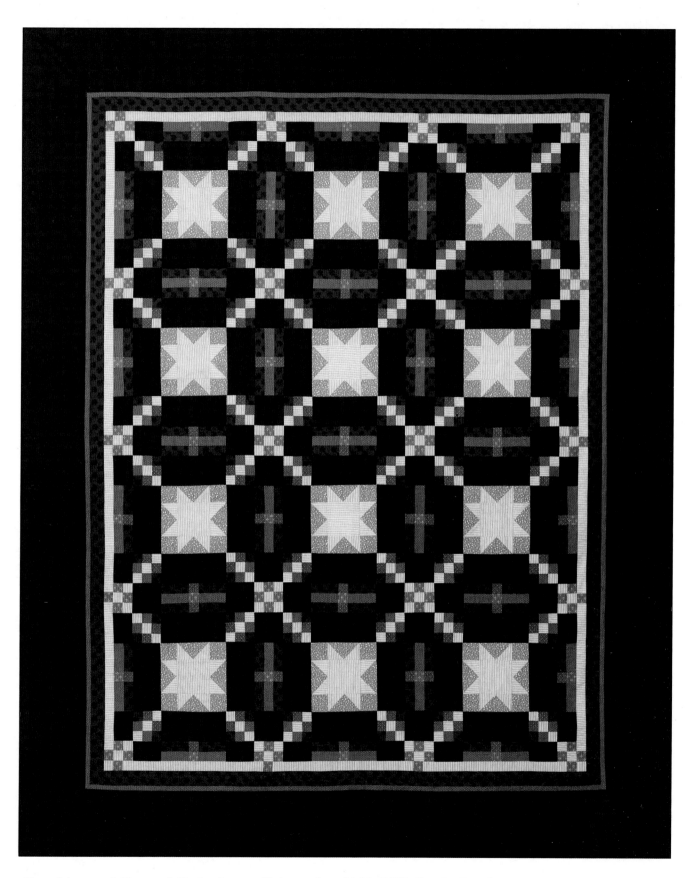

Sunshine and Grape Jelly by Laura Reinstatler, 1988, Mill Creek, Washington, 71" x 86". Derived from the same line drawing as the two versions of Starlight Surrounded shown on the opposite page, this quilt is a wonderful example of how different quilters view the same design.

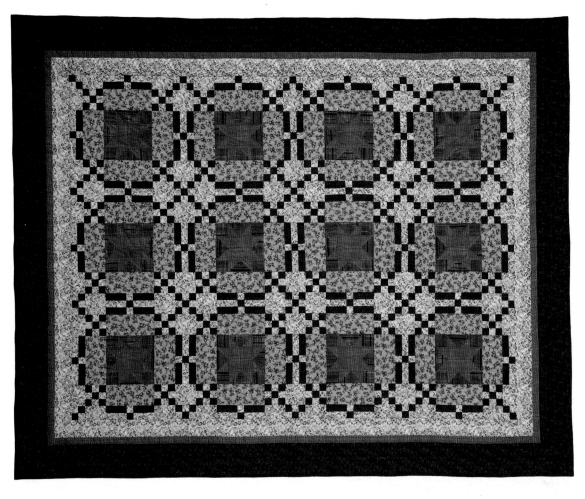

Starlight Surrounded by Marsha McCloskey, 1989, Seattle, Washington, 81" x 65". This design is a combination of two traditional patchwork designs, Burgoyne Surrounded and the Sawtooth Star. Quilted by Virginia Lauth.

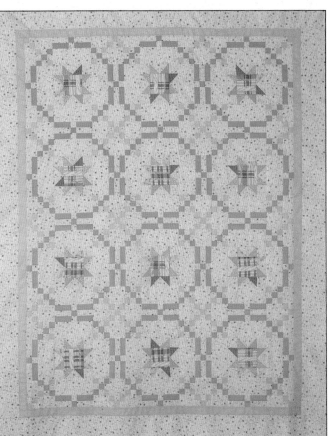

Starlight Surrounded by Joan Hanson, 1988, Seattle, Washington, 66" x 82". The large-scale designer print used for the stars and the low-contrast Ninepatch units give this interpretation of the design a soft look.

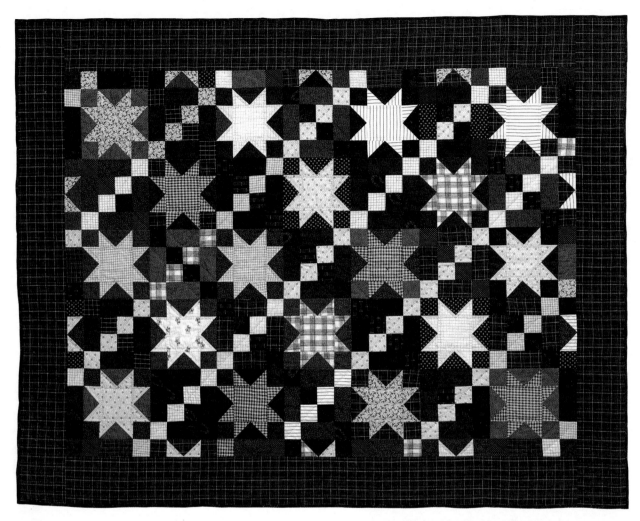

Stars and Stepping Stones by Marsha McCloskey, 1988, Seattle, Washington, 71" x 55". Stepping-stone blocks form two chains of squares that diagonally frame Sawtooth Stars in this two-block design. Quilted by Virginia Lauth.

Stepping Stones by Carolann Palmer, 1989, Seattle, Washington, 86" x 102". Worked here in classic blue and white, this traditional design is also known as Arrowheads or Blackford's Beauty.

Cranberry Relish by Judy Pollard, 1988, Seattle, Washington, 75 1/2" x 66 1/2". Alternating background prints add interest as two-colored Le Moyne Stars are framed by rows of cranberry squares. Quilted by Virginia Lauth.

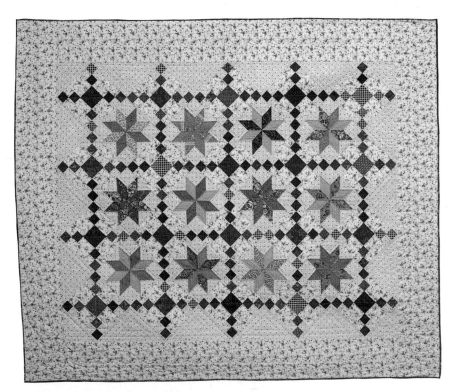

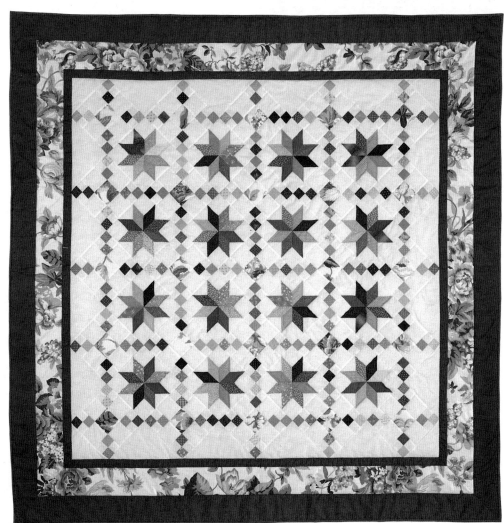

Blueberry Shortcake by Cleo Nolette, 1989, Seattle, Washington, 81" x 81". This pattern is made of two traditional designs, the Le Moyne Star and the Single Irish Chain, and is an alternate coloring of Cranberry Relish, also shown on this page.

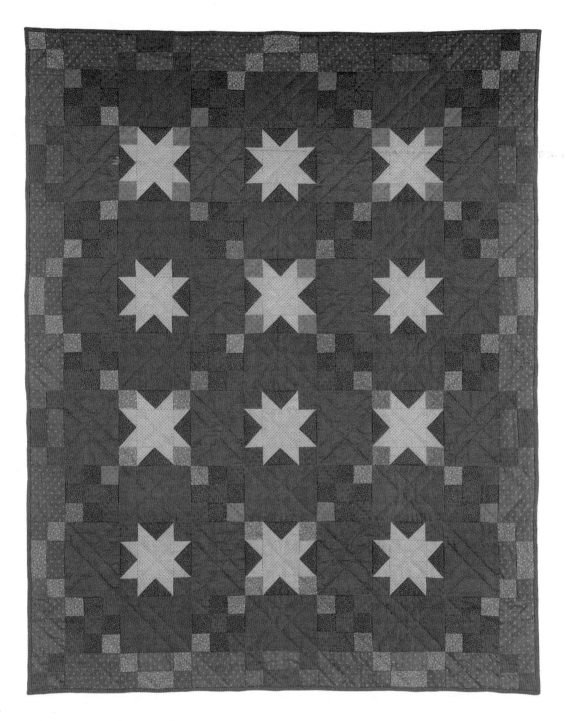

Star Matrix by Marsha McCloskey, 1989, Seattle, Washington, 42" x 62 ½".
Two sets of stepping stones, one that comes forward visually and one that
recedes, link bright yellow stars on a green background.
Quilted by Virginia Lauth.

Quilt Patterns

Instructions for eight Stars and Stepping Stones quilts can be found in this section. For each quilt, you will find a materials list, complete step-by-step directions, and a design work sheet (Quilt Diagram) to help you make design changes, if you wish. A color photograph of each quilt can be found in the Gallery section that begins on page 29.

Cutting specifications geared for rotary cutting are given in the directions, with a template reference. Templates are found on pages 55–61. Use them to check the accuracy of your rotary cutting or for hand cutting and piecing, if you prefer a more traditional approach. All measurements include the ¼" seam allowance. DO NOT ADD SEAM ALLOWANCES TO THE DIMENSIONS GIVEN.

Cutting specifications for triangles indicate the size of the square from which the triangles will be cut (see pages 19–20). Directions for half-square triangles are "cut diagonally," while directions for quarter-square triangles are "cut twice diagonally." Set triangles for diagonally set blocks are cut as quarter-square triangles.

Before you begin, read the complete cutting and piecing directions for the quilt you are going to make. Quick cutting with the rotary cutter is discussed on pages 15–20. Refer to pages 21–24 for tips on machine piecing and strip piecing. Consult the Glossary of Techniques on pages 62–64 for complete directions on quilt finishing techniques, including borders and binding.

Stars and Stepping Stones

A color photo of this quilt is on page 34. It is a two-block design that is easy to rotary cut and machine piece.

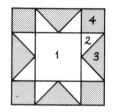

Sawtooth Star, 8"
Piece 18

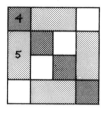

Alternate block, 8"
Piece 17

Border Unit #1
Piece 10

Border Unit #2
Piece 14

Corners
Cut 4

DIMENSIONS: 55" x 71"

MATERIALS: (45" wide fabric)

Dark: 1⅝ yds. total assorted maroon prints and plaids for star backgrounds, border units, and alternate blocks

Light: 1½ yds. total assorted light background fabric with navy or maroon figures for stars and light chains

Accent: ½ yd. total assorted navy prints and plaids for dark chains

Border: 2⅛ yds. maroon plaid

Backing: 3¼ yds.

Batting, binding, and thread to finish

CUTTING

1. From the border fabric, cut and set aside four 6" wide strips the length of the fabric. These strips are longer than needed and will be trimmed to fit later.
2. Cut 18 squares, 4½" x 4½", of assorted light fabrics for star centers (Template #1).
3. Cut 82 squares, 2⅞" x 2⅞", of assorted light fabrics. Cut diagonally to yield 164 half-square triangles for star points (Template #2).
4. Cut 21 squares, 5¼" x 5¼", of assorted dark fabrics. Cut squares twice diagonally to yield 82 quarter-square triangles for star backgrounds and border units (Template #3).
5. Cut 106 squares, 2½" x 2½", of assorted dark fabrics for star backgrounds and border units (Template #4).
6. Cut 82 squares, 2½" x 2½", of light fabrics and 82 squares, 2½" x 2½", of navy fabrics for alternate blocks (Template #4).
7. Cut 82 rectangles, 2½" x 4½", of assorted dark fabrics for alternate blocks and border units (Template #5).

DIRECTIONS

1. Piece 18 Sawtooth Star blocks. See page 25 for special piecing instructions.
2. Piece 17 alternate blocks. See page 24 for strip-piecing technique.
3. Piece 10 Border Unit #1 and 14 Border Unit #2. Set aside 4 dark 2½" squares for corner pieces (Template #4).
4. Join Sawtooth Stars, alternate blocks, border units, and corner squares together in appropriate rows, as shown. Make two Row 1 for top and bottom of quilt. Make four Row 2 and three Row 3. Join rows to complete pieced section of quilt.

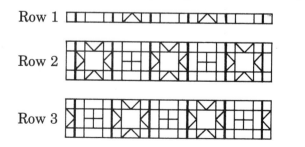

5. Stitch 6" wide border strips to quilt center, using either blunt-sewn or mitered corners.
6. Add batting and backing; quilt.
7. Finish edges with bias binding.

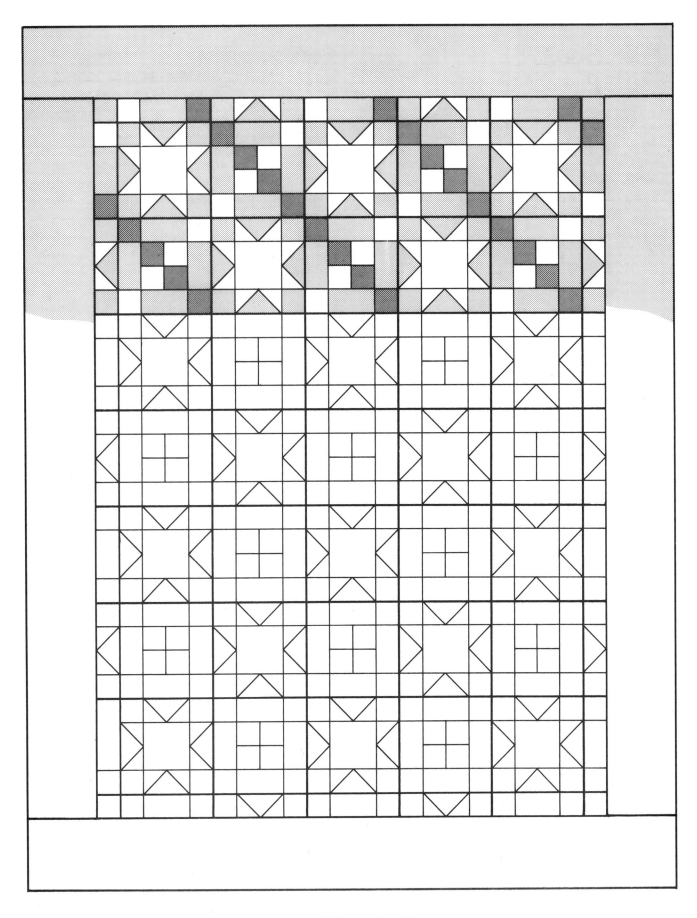

Stars and Stepping Stones

Star Matrix

Star Matrix features two overlaid sets of stepping stones. In the quilt pictured on page 36, the intention was to make the lavender chains of squares appear to recede and the red chains to advance. The yellow stars contrast well with both sets of chaining squares and the green background.

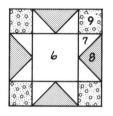

Sawtooth Star I, 6"
Piece 6

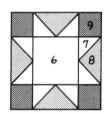

Sawtooth Star II, 6"
Piece 6

Border Unit I
Piece 7

Border Unit II
Piece 7

Four Patch I
Piece 2

Four Patch II
Piece 2

Ninepatch
Piece 20

11
Cut 31

12
Cut 18

DIMENSIONS: 42" x 62½"

MATERIALS: (45" wide fabric)

Star color: ⅝ yd. gold
First chain of squares: ½ yd. lavender
Second chain of squares: ½ yd. red
Background: 1½ yds. green
Backing: 1⅞ yds.
Batting, binding, and thread to finish

CUTTING

1. Cut 12 squares, 3½" x 3½", of star color for star centers (Template #6).
2. Cut 48 squares, 2⅜" x 2⅜", of star color. Cut diagonally to yield 96 half-square triangles for star points (Template #7).
3. Cut 12 squares, 4¼" x 4¼", of background color. Cut twice diagonally to yield 48 quarter-square triangles for star backgrounds (Template #8).
4. Cut 102 squares, 2" x 2", of first chain color for corners of Sawtooth Star I, Ninepatches, Border Unit I, and Four Patch I (Template #9).
5. Cut 85 squares, 2" x 2", of second chain color for corners of Sawtooth Star II, Ninepatches, Border Unit II, and Four Patch II (Template #9).
6. Cut 116 squares, 2" x 2", of background color for Ninepatches, border units, and Four Patches (Template #9).
7. Cut 7 rectangles, 2" x 3½", of first chain color and 7 rectangles, 2" x 3½", of second chain color for border units (Template #10).
8. Cut 14 rectangles, 2 x 3½", of background color for border units (Template #10).
9. Cut 31 rectangles, 5" x 6½" (Template #11), and 18 rectangles, 3½" x 5", of background color for set pieces (Template #12).

DIRECTIONS

1. Piece 6 Sawtooth Star I with corners of the first chain color and 6 Sawtooth Star II with corners of the second chain color. Instructions for piecing the Sawtooth Star are on page 25.
2. Piece 20 Ninepatches with 2 squares of the first chain color, 3 squares of the second chain color, and 4 squares of the background color. Refer to page 24 for strip-piecing techniques to make Ninepatches, Four Patches, and border units.
3. Piece 7 Border Unit I (first chain color and background); 7 Border Unit II (second chain color and background); 2 Four Patch I (first chain color and background); and 2 Four Patch II (second chain color and background).
4. Arrange all pieced blocks and units with the #11 and #12 set pieces in rows, as pictured in quilt diagram. Pay close attention to color arrangement. Make two Row 1 for top and bottom of quilt; three Row 2; two Row 3; two Row 4; and two Row 5. Sew rows together to complete quilt top.
5. Add backing and batting; quilt.
6. Finish edges with bias binding.

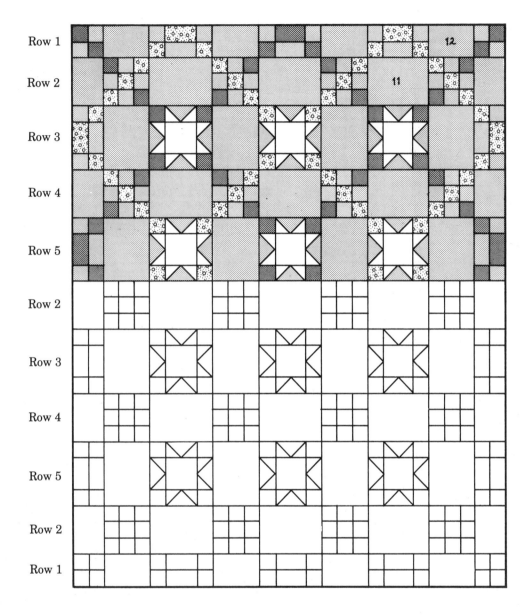

Star Matrix

Irish Beauty

This combination of two traditional patterns, the Le Moyne Star and Double Irish Chain, is shown in two versions in the Gallery on page 29.

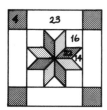

Block A, 10"
Piece 6

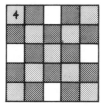

Block B, 10"
Piece 2

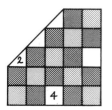

Section C
Piece 6

Section D
Piece 4

Section E
Piece 2

DIMENSIONS: 42" x 56"

MATERIALS: (45" wide fabric)

Light: ⅝ yd. light blue print for star background and piecing chains

Medium: 1¾ yds. blue plaid for piecing stars and chains and borders

Dark: 1 yd. blue print for piecing stars and chains

Backing: 1¾ yds.

Batting, binding, and thread to finish

CUTTING

1. Cut 4½" wide strips from the length of the medium fabric for borders and set aside. Extra length will be trimmed later.
2. Cut 24 squares, 2¼" x 2¼", of light fabric for star backgrounds (Template #16).
3. Cut 6 squares, 3¾" x 3¾", of light fabric. Cut twice diagonally to yield 24 quarter-square triangles for star backgrounds (Template #14).

4. Cut 24 diamonds from dark fabric and 24 diamonds from medium fabric (Template #22). See page 20 for rotary cutting this shape.
5. Cut 24 rectangles, 2½" x 6½", of light fabric for Block A (Template #23).
6. Cut 100 squares, 2½" x 2½", of dark fabric (Template #4); 80 squares, 2½" x 2½", of medium fabric; and 24 squares, 2½" x 2½", of light fabric. These squares will be used in piecing units A, B, C, D, and E.
7. Cut 11 squares, 4¹⁄₁₆" x 4¹⁄₁₆", of light fabric. Cut twice diagonally to yield 44 quarter-square triangles for outer edges of sections C, D, and E (Template #2).
8. Cut 2 squares, 2⁵⁄₁₆" x 2⁵⁄₁₆", of light fabric. Cut diagonally to yield 4 half-square triangles for corner piece of Section D (Template #24).

DIRECTIONS

1. Piece 6 Block A. Refer to page 26 for instructions on piecing the Le Moyne Star.
2. Make 2 Block B; 6 Section C; 4 Section D; and 2 Section E.
3. Arrange blocks and sections in the quilt design according to the piecing diagram. Sew diagonal rows together and add the corner section, Unit D, last.

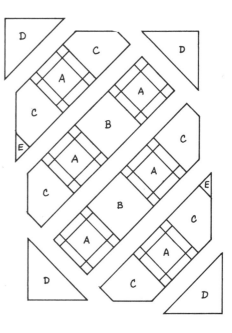

4. Add 4½" wide border strips, using either blunt-sewn or mitered corners.
5. Add batting and backing; quilt.
6. Finish edges with bias binding.

Irish Beauty

Cranberry Relish

Judy Pollard's version of this Le Moyne Star and Single Irish Chain design can be found on page 35. Cleo Nolette's interpretation of the same pattern, which she calls Blueberry Shortcake, is also on page 35.

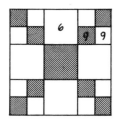

Single Irish Chain, 9"
Piece 20

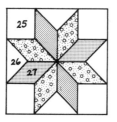

Le Moyne Star, 9"
Piece 12

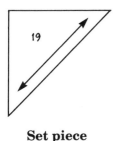

Set piece
Cut 14

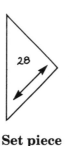

Set piece
Cut 4

DIMENSIONS: 66½" x 75½"

MATERIALS: (45" wide fabric)

Light: 2¾ yds. total assorted light prints with pink or blue figures for block backgrounds
Medium: 1 yd. total assorted medium blue and reddish prints for stars
Dark: ¾ yd. total assorted red prints for Single Irish Chain blocks
Border: 2¼ yds.
Backing: 3⅝ yds.
Batting, binding, and thread to finish

CUTTING

Note: Rotary cutting dimensions for the 9" Le Moyne Star block are not given here, because the measurements do not easily correspond to standard rulers. To cut these pieces using rotary methods, take your dimensions from the templates or make paper templates and tape them to the bottom side of your ruler, as suggested on page 14.

1. Cut 4 border strips 8½" wide from the length of the border fabric and set aside. Extra length will be trimmed later.
2. Using Template #25, cut 48 squares of light fabric for Le Moyne Star backgrounds.
3. Using Template #26, cut 48 triangles of light fabric for Le Moyne Star backgrounds.
4. Using Template #27, cut 96 diamonds of assorted medium prints for Le Moyne Star blocks.
5. Cut 20 squares, 3½" x 3½", of assorted dark fabric and 80 squares, 3½" x 3½", of light background fabric for Single Irish Chain blocks (Template #6).
6. Cut 160 squares, 2" x 2", of assorted dark fabrics and 160 squares, 2" x 2", of light background fabric for Single Irish Chain blocks (Template #9).
7. Cut 4 squares, 14" x 14", of light background fabric. Cut twice diagonally to yield 14 quarter-square triangles for side set pieces (Template #19).
8. Cut 2 squares, 7¼" x 7¼", of light background fabric. Cut diagonally to yield 4 half-square triangles for corner set pieces (Template #28).

DIRECTIONS

1. Piece 12 Le Moyne Star blocks. Special instructions for piecing this block are on page 26.
2. Piece 20 Single Irish Chain blocks. Refer to page 24 for strip piecing the Four Patches.
3. Arrange pieced Le Moyne Star and Single Irish Chain blocks in diagonal rows with set pieces #19 and #28, as shown in quilt diagram. Sew blocks together in rows, then join rows together to complete center pieced section.
4. Sew 8½" border strips to pieced center section, using either blunt-sewn or mitered corners.
5. Add batting and backing; quilt.
6. Finish edges with bias binding.

Cranberry Relish

Stepping Stones

This pattern is the traditional Stepping Stones design. Carolann Palmer's classic blue-and-white version is pictured on page 34.

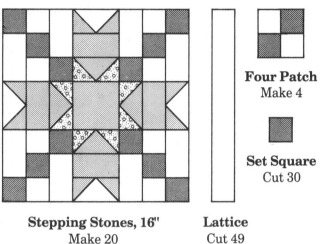

Stepping Stones, 16"
Make 20

Lattice
Cut 49

Four Patch
Make 4

Set Square
Cut 30

DIMENSIONS: 86" x 102"

MATERIALS: (45" wide fabric)

Dark: 1⅝ yds. navy blue for piecing blocks, set squares, and pieced border

Medium: 2⅜ yds. medium blue for blocks and pieced borders

Light: 1 yd. light blue for piecing blocks and border

Background: 5½ yds. for block backgrounds, lattices, and plain border

Backing: 6 yds.

Batting, binding, and thread to finish

CUTTING

1. Cut a 3-yard length of background fabric for the plain borders and lattice strips. From this length, cut 4 strips 4½" wide and 9 strips 2½" wide. Set the 4½" wide strips aside for borders; extra length will be trimmed later. From the 2½" wide strips, cut 49 lattice sections that measure 16½".
2. Cut 160 squares, 2½" x 2½", of background fabric for pieced blocks (Template #4).
3. Cut 160 rectangles, 2½" x 4½", of background fabric for pieced blocks (Template #5).
4. Cut 20 squares, 5¼" x 5¼", of background fabric. Cut twice diagonally to yield 80 quarter-square triangles for pieced blocks (Template #3).
5. Cut 340 squares, 2½" x 2½", of dark fabric for pieced blocks, set squares, corner Four Patches, and pieced borders (Template #4).
6. Cut 20 squares, 4½" x 4½", of medium fabric for pieced blocks (Template #1).
7. Cut 80 rectangles, 2½" x 4½", from medium fabric for pieced blocks (Template #5).
8. Cut 62 squares, 2½" x 2½", of medium fabric for pieced borders (Template #4).
9. Cut 20 squares, 5¼" x 5¼", of medium fabric. Cut twice diagonally to yield 80 quarter-square triangles for pieced blocks (Template #3).
10. Cut 80 squares, 2⅞" x 2⅞", from medium fabric. Cut once diagonally to yield 160 half-square triangles for pieced blocks (Template #2).
11. Cut 62 squares, 2½" x 2½", of light fabric for pieced borders (Template #4).
12. Cut 80 squares, 2⅞" x 2⅞", of light fabric. Cut once diagonally to yield 160 half-square triangles for pieced blocks (Template #2).

DIRECTIONS

1. Piece 20 Stepping Stones blocks. Refer to page 24 for strip piecing the corner sections.
2. Sew completed blocks, lattice strips, and dark set squares (Template #4) together in rows, as shown in the quilt diagram. Join rows together to complete pieced center section.
3. Make 4 corner Four Patch units.
4. Trim 4½" wide border strips to fit the long sides of the center section. Cut the other 2 strips to fit the width of the center section. To these 2 shorter strips, add the corner Four Patch units. Sew the long strips to the sides of the quilt; then sew the shorter strips-with-Four-Patches to the top and bottom.
5. For the pieced border, sew squares (Template #4) together in rows, following a light, medium, dark color order. Make a strip 49 squares long for each side of the quilt; make a strip 43 squares long for the top and another for the bottom. Sew pieced borders to quilt sides first, then to the top and bottom.
6. Add batting and backing; quilt.
7. Finish edges with bias binding.

Stepping Stones

The Great Unknown

The Great Unknown combines two traditional designs: the Unknown Star and the Single Irish Chain. In Nancy J. Martin's version of this quilt, pictured on page 31, the outer Single Irish Chain blocks are colored differently to create a mock-pieced border.

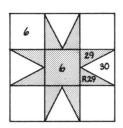

Unknown Star, 9"
Piece 12

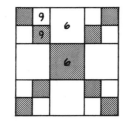

Single Irish Chain I, 9"
(alternate block)
Piece 6

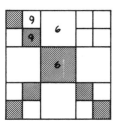

Single Irish Chain II, 9"
(side block)
Piece 10

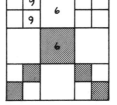

Single Irish Chain III, 9"
(corner block)
Piece 4

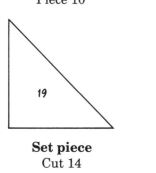

Set piece
Cut 14

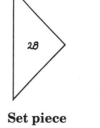

Set piece
Cut 4

DIMENSIONS: 51" x 63½"

MATERIALS: (45" wide fabric)
Dark A: ¾ yd. total assorted green prints for stars
Dark B: ¾ yd. total assorted brown and maroon prints for Irish chains
Background: 3 yds. total assorted pink prints
Backing: 3 yds.
Batting, binding, and thread to finish

CUTTING

1. Cut 12 squares, 3½" x 3½", of Dark A for star blocks (Template #6); 128 squares, 3½" x 3½", of assorted background fabrics for use in all blocks; and 20 squares, 3½" x 3½", of Dark B for Single Irish Chain blocks.
2. Using Template #29, cut 48 triangles plus 48 triangles reversed of Dark A.
3. Using Template #30, cut 48 triangles of assorted background fabrics for star blocks.
4. Cut 124 squares, 2" x 2", of Dark B (Template #9) and 196 squares, 2" x 2", of assorted background fabrics for Irish Chain blocks.
5. Cut 4 squares, 14" x 14", of assorted background fabrics. Cut twice diagonally to yield 14 quarter-square triangles for outside edge set pieces (Template #19).
6. Cut 2 squares, 7¼" x 7¼", of background fabrics. Cut diagonally to yield 4 half-square triangles for corner set pieces (Template #28).

DIRECTIONS

1. Piece 12 Unknown Star blocks. Special instructions for piecing this block are on page 28.
2. There are 3 different colorings of the Single Irish Chain block in this quilt. Cut and piece 6 alternate blocks, 10 side blocks, and 4 corner blocks. Study the illustration for color placement. Refer to page 24 for instructions on strip piecing the Four Patch units.
3. Arrange pieced Unknown Star blocks and Single Irish Chain blocks with set pieces #19 and #28 in diagonal rows, as shown. Pay close attention to block coloration and orientation. Sew blocks together in rows, then join the rows to complete the quilt top.
4. Add batting and backing; quilt.
5. Finish edges with bias binding.

The Great Unknown

Fifty-four-Forty or Fight

Fifty-four-Forty or Fight is a traditional block design. Lattices and set squares in the same scale as the small squares in the block continue the two sets of diagonal chains that travel across the quilt. The use of many fabrics and varying contrasts gives this quilt sparkle, which you can see in the top color photograph on page 30.

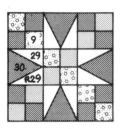

Fifty-four-Forty or Fight, 9"
Piece 12

Second chain square
Cut 20

Lattice strip
Cut 31

DIMENSIONS: 45" x 53"

MATERIALS: (45" wide fabric)

Light: ½ yd. total assorted gray prints for star points

Medium A: ⅜ yd. total assorted maroon prints for first chain

Medium B: ½ yd. total assorted green prints for second chain

Dark: 1 yd. total assorted black prints and plaids for background and lattices

Borders: ¾ yd. total assorted black prints
    ¼ yd. maroon print

Backing: 1⅝ yds.

Batting, binding, and thread to finish

CUTTING

1. Using Template #29, cut 48 triangles plus 48 triangles reversed of assorted light fabrics.
2. Using Template #30, cut 48 triangles of assorted dark background fabrics for star blocks.
3. Cut 96 squares, 2" x 2", of assorted dark background fabrics (Template #9); cut 72 squares, 2" x 2", of Medium A for the first chain and 92 squares, 2" x 2", of Medium B for the second chain.
4. Cut 31 lattice strips, 2" x 9½", from assorted dark background fabrics.
5. The borders for this quilt were constructed from scraps, so use what you have to add border sections to bring the quilt out to the desired finished size. Cut the following if you want to make the borders as shown:
   a. Cut and piece two 3½" x 33½" borders from assorted black fabrics.
   b. Cut two 5" x 50" borders from black print fabric.
   c. Cut two 2½" x 45" borders from maroon fabric.

DIRECTIONS

1. Piece 12 Fifty-four-Forty or Fight blocks. Refer to the instructions for piecing the Unknown Star on page 28, and to strip piecing Four Patches on page 24.
2. Set blocks, lattice strips, and remaining second chain squares (20) together with the pieced blocks in rows. Stitch rows together to complete pieced center of quilt.
3. Add 3½" x 33½" pieced borders to top and bottom of quilt. Stitch 5" x 50" borders to sides. Add 2½" x 45" borders to top and bottom; or add borders of your choice.
4. Add batting and backing; quilt.
5. Finish edges with bias binding.

Fifty-four-Forty or Fight

Starlight Surrounded

Three versions of this quilt appear in the Gallery on pages 32–33. Quilt directions given here are for the quilt that appears on top of page 33. Color arrangement and emphasis can change the design dramatically.

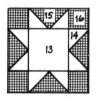

Sawtooth Star, 7"
Piece 12

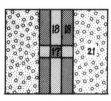

Unit A
Piece 17

Unit B
Piece 6

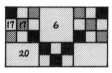

Unit C
Piece 10

Unit D
Piece 14

Unit E
Piece 4

DIMENSIONS: 65" x 81"

MATERIALS: (45" wide fabric)

Light: 2⅓ yds. gray for inner border and piecing
Medium A: 1 yd. gray for Template #21
Medium B: ½ yd. gray plaid for star backgrounds
Dark A: 2⅓ yds. black for outer border and piecing
Dark B: ¾ yd. maroon for piecing
Accent: 1¼ yds. pink for stars and middle border
Backing: 3¾ yds.
Batting, binding, and thread to finish

CUTTING

1. Cut the following strips for borders from the lengthwise grain of fabric. These dimensions include extra length for eacy mitering and will need to be trimmed to fit:
   Inner border (light): Cut 2 strips, 3" x 67", and 2 strips, 3" x 83".
   Middle border (accent): Cut 2 strips, 1½" x 67", and 2 strips, 1½" x 83".
   Outer border (Dark A): Cut 2 strips, 5" x 67", and 2 strips, 5" x 83".
2. Cut 12 squares, 4" x 4", of accent fabric for star centers (Template #13).
3. Cut 48 squares, 2⅝" x 2⅝", of accent fabric. Cut diagonally to yield 96 half-square triangles for star points (Template #14).
4. Cut 12 squares, 4¾" x 4¾", of Medium B. Cut twice diagonally to yield 48 quarter-square triangles for star backgrounds (Template #15).
5. Cut 48 squares, 2¼" x 2¼", of Medium B for star backgrounds (Template #16).
6. Cut 242 squares, 1½" x 1½", of light background fabric (Template #17). Cut 175 squares, 1½" x 1½", of Dark B and 164 of Dark A.
7. Cut 68 rectangles, 1½" x 3½", of light fabric (Template #18). Cut 72 rectangles, 1½" x 3½", of Dark B. These pieces are for the rectangle units.
8. Cut 34 squares, 3½" x 3½", of light fabric (Template #6). Cut 28 rectangles, 2½" x 3½", of light fabric (Template #20).
9. Cut 48 rectangles, 3½" x 7½", of Medium A (Template #21).

DIRECTIONS

1. Piece 12 Star blocks. Instructions for piecing the Sawtooth Star are on page 25.
2. Make 48 Ninepatch I with 3 squares of Dark B, 2 squares of Dark A, and 4 squares of light fabric; 6 Ninepatch II with 5 squares of Dark A and 4 squares of light fabric; 10 Six Patches with 3 squares of Dark A and 3 squares of light fabric; 4 Four Patches with 2 squares of Dark A and 2 squares of light fabric; 17 Rectangle I with 1 square of Dark B, 2 squares of light fabric, 2 rectangles of light fabric, and 4 rectangles of Dark B; and 14 Rectangle II with 1 square each of Dark A and light fabric, and 2 rectangles each of Dark A and light fabric. **Note:** Even though the cutting instructions give rotary cutting and template designations, it is easiest to piece

Starlight Surrounded

these units by sewing 1½" strips together in strata and subcutting to appropriate dimensions (see page 24 for strip-piecing instructions).

Ninepatch I
Piece 48

Ninepatch II
Piece 6

Six Patch
Piece 10

Four Patch
Piece 4

Rectangle I
Piece 17

Rectangle II
Piece 14

3. Combine the units made in step 2 into larger units, as shown. Make 17 Unit A, 6 Unit B, 10 Unit C, 14 Unit D, and 4 Unit E.

4. Arrange units A–E in rows with star blocks, according to the quilt diagram. Make two Row 1 for quilt top and bottom, make four Row 2; make three Row 3. Sew rows together in order shown to complete quilt center.

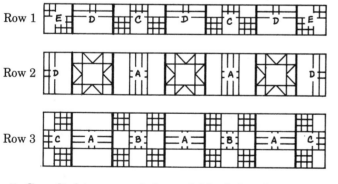

Row 1

Row 2

Row 3

5. Sew light gray, pink, and black border strips together in preparation for mitering. Stitch to quilt center and miter corners as discussed on pages 62–63.

6. Add batting and backing; quilt.

7. Finish edges with bias binding.

Templates

In order to accommodate the work methods of as many quilters as possible, templates in this section are offered in a multiuse form. Each shape has a number, which is referenced in the quilt directions. The inner dashed line is the sewing line; the outer solid line is the cutting line and includes the ¼" seam allowance. Essential finished or sewn dimensions are indicated just inside the sewing line; cutting dimensions are indicated just outside the cutting line. Quick-cutting configurations and dimensions are given for all half-square and quarter-square triangles.

Triangle points have been left on to aid in measuring for rotary cutting, but lines show where to cut off the points for easiest matching.

For hand piecing, where a drawn sewing line is desired, carefully trace each shape on graph paper or tracing paper, using the sewing line as your guide. Glue the paper shape to template plastic and cut out accurately; you now have a template to trace around for hand piecing. If you use templates that include seam allowances, trace on the outer or cutting line.

If you prefer using a ruler and rotary cutter, use the measurements provided with each shape for cutting and compare your patches to the templates in the book to check for accuracy. You can also use these measurements for strip piecing squares and rectangles (see page 24).

Grain lines are for lengthwise or crosswise grain and are shown with an arrow on each piece. Because of space limitations, some of the larger templates are half templates, with fold lines indicated. Make sure the other half of the pattern is accurate, when making one of these larger templates. Detailed directions for using templates are on pages 13–14.

Note: Smaller pieces overlap larger pieces, so be sure to draw the entire template, including the space covered by the smaller piece, when you make the larger template.

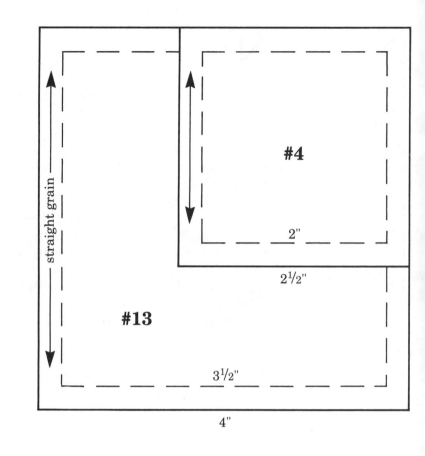

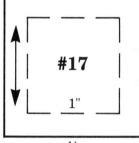

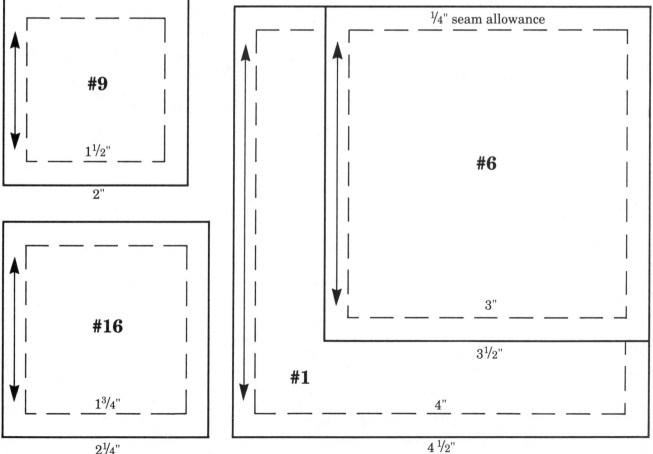

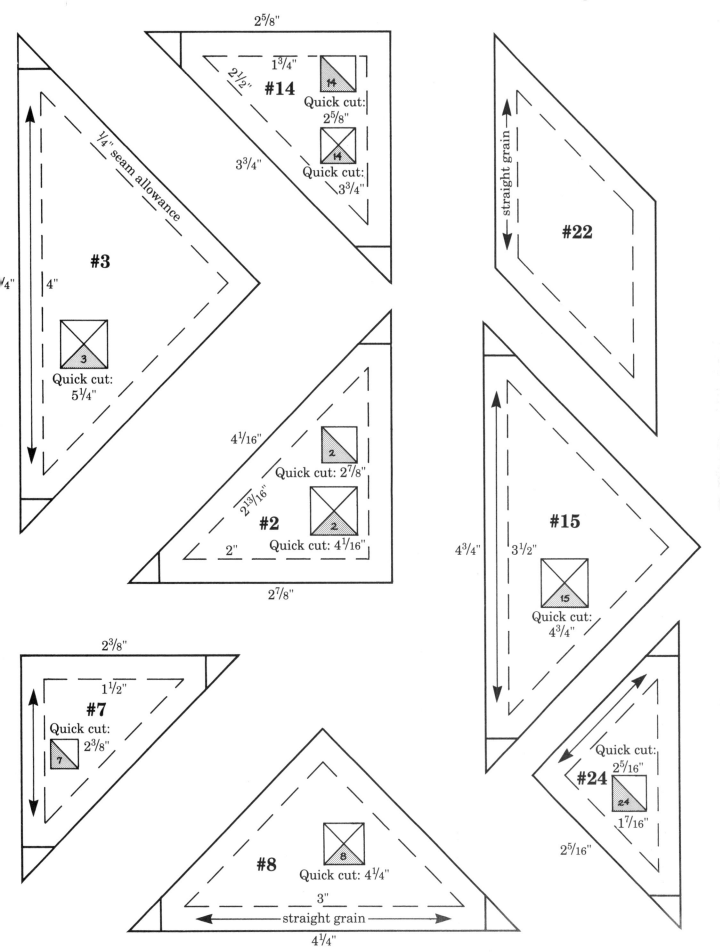

#14

2⁵/₈"

1³/₄"

2¹/₂"

3³/₄"

Quick cut:
2⁵/₈"

Quick cut:
3³/₄"

#3

¼" seam allowance

4"

Quick cut:
5¼"

#22

straight grain

#2

4¹/₁₆"

Quick cut: 2⁷/₈"

2¹³/₁₆"

Quick cut: 4¹/₁₆"

2"

2⁷/₈"

#15

4³/₄"

3½"

Quick cut:
4³/₄"

#7

2³/₈"

1½"

Quick cut:
2³/₈"

#24

Quick cut:
2⁵/₁₆"

1⁷/₁₆"

2⁵/₁₆"

#8

Quick cut: 4¼"

3"

straight grain

4¼"

Note: Smaller pieces overlap larger pieces, so be sure to draw the entire template, including the space covered by the smaller piece, when you make the larger template.

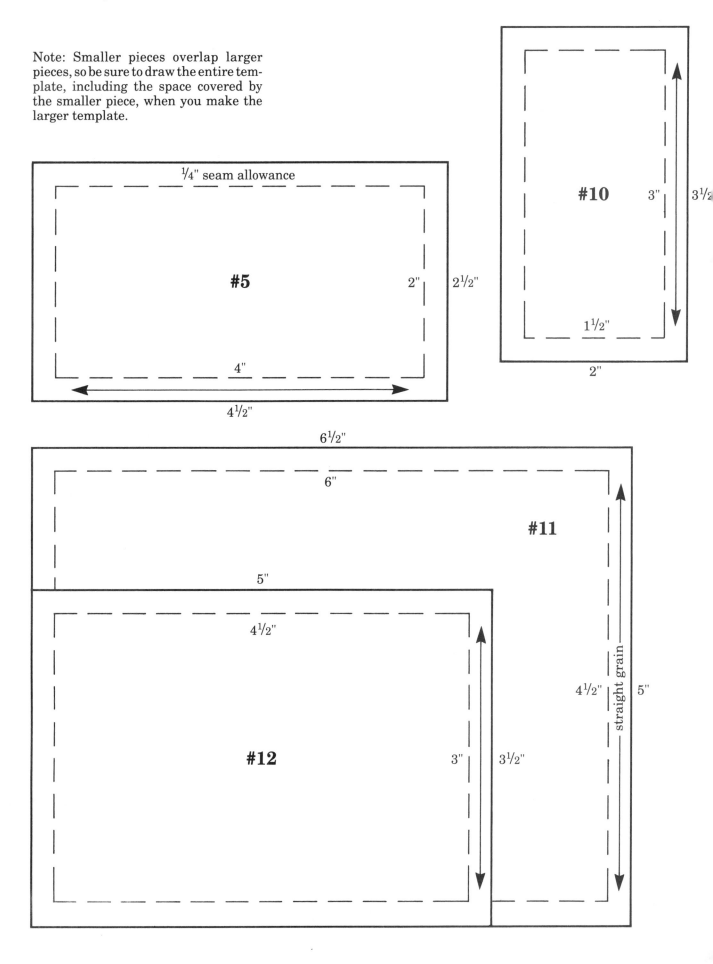

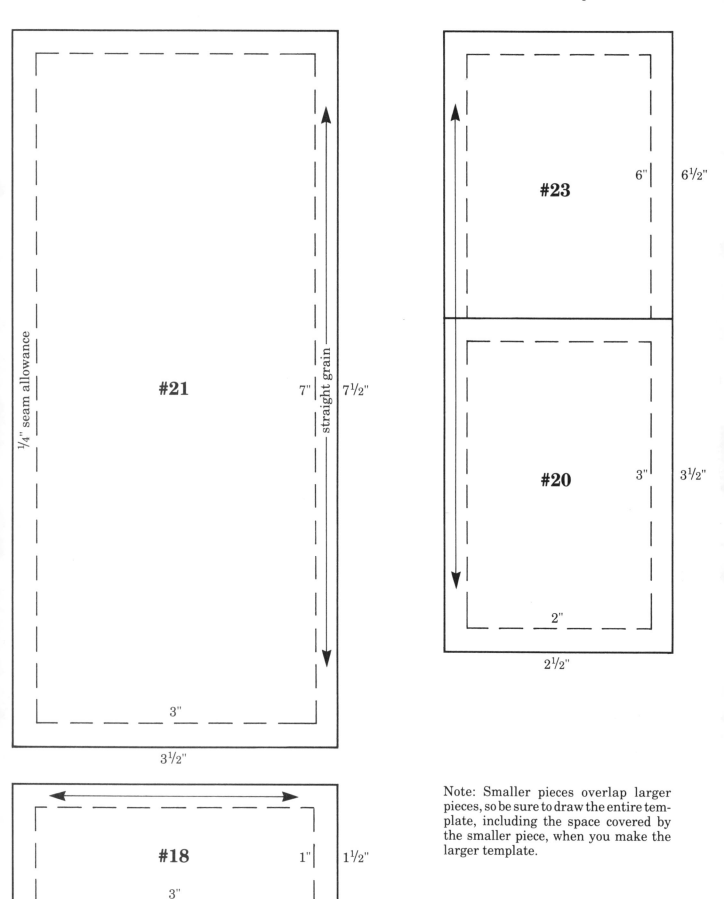

#21

¼" seam allowance

straight grain

7"   7½"

3"

3½"

#23

6"   6½"

#20

3"   3½"

2"

2½"

#18

1"   1½"

3"

3½"

Note: Smaller pieces overlap larger pieces, so be sure to draw the entire template, including the space covered by the smaller piece, when you make the larger template.

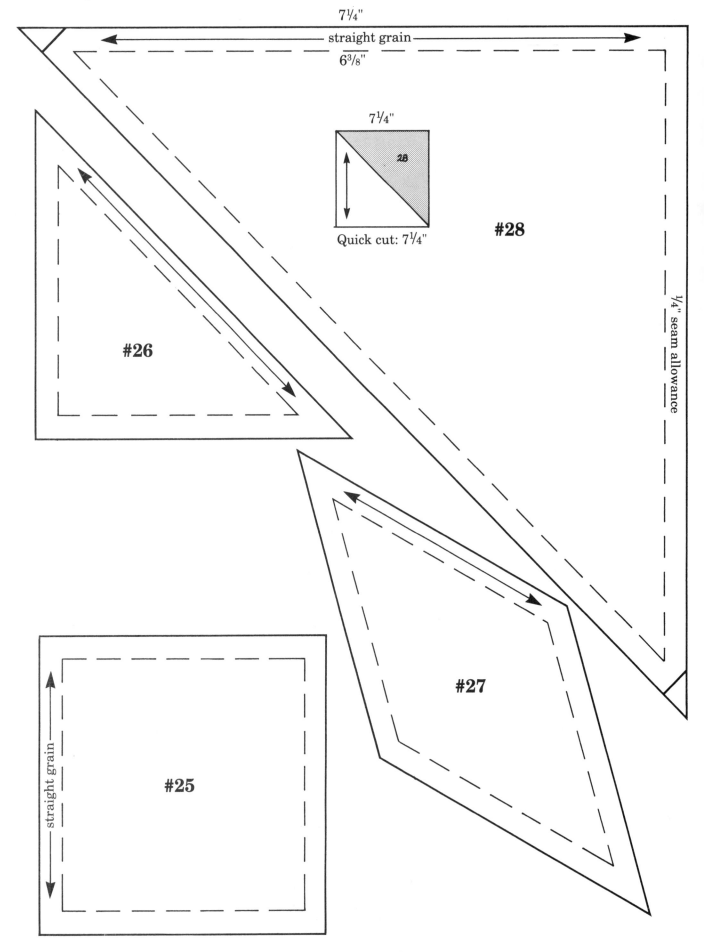

7¼"
straight grain
6³⁄₈"

7¼"

28

Quick cut: 7¼"

#28

¼" seam allowance

#26

#27

straight grain

#25

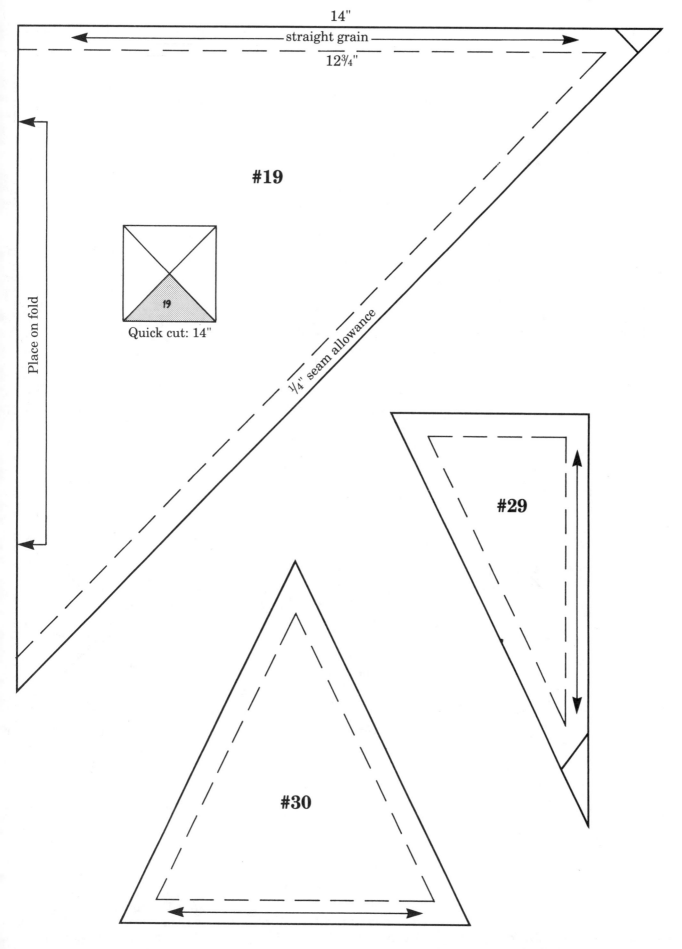

14"
straight grain
12¾"

#19

f9

Quick cut: 14"

Place on fold

¼" seam allowance

#29

#30

Glossary of Techniques

Assembling the Quilt Top

When all of the blocks are pieced, you are ready to "set" the quilt top together. Following a setting plan, first stitch together blocks, or blocks and lattices, into rows with ¼" seams. Then, stitch together rows of blocks, or blocks and lattice strips. Setting sequences are shown in piecing diagrams with the individual quilt directions.

Assembly sequence of diagonally set quilt

Assembly sequence with lattices

Borders

Borders function as a frame for a quilt design. For plain borders with straight-sewn corners, first sew borders to the long sides of the quilt, then to the short sides. Striped fabrics make lovely quilt borders, but the corners must be mitered to make the design turn the corner gracefully. Mitered corners are not difficult to do and are worth the effort in some design situations. Miter corners when using stripes or multiple plain borders.

You will need to buy fabric the length of the longest outside border, plus about 4" to allow for shrinkage. It is often wise, when cutting border strips, to leave them 3" to 4" longer than the length given in the pattern. When the actual dimensions of the quilt top are known, the border strips can be trimmed to fit.

Always cut border strips from yardage before you cut the patches to ensure that you have continuous yardage. If you need to piece border strips, press seams open and place in the center of each side of the quilt for minimum visibility. If you are using a striped border, it is best not to piece it.

Always measure the length and width through the center of the quilt top to determine border dimensions. (Outside edges may have stretched or be distorted.) Pin borders to quilt top evenly, easing in any fullness on top or border. Stitch together with a ¼" seam.

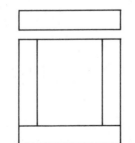

Borders with blunt-sewn corners

Mitering Corners

1. Prepare the borders. Determine the finished outside dimension of your quilt. Cut the borders this length, plus 3" or 4" for seam allowances and ease of matching. When using a striped fabric for borders, make sure the design on all four sides is cut the same way. Sew multiple border strips together first and treat the resulting "striped" units as a single border for mitering.

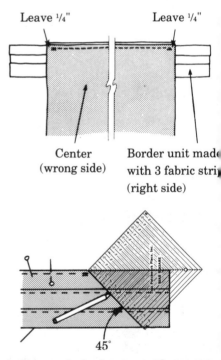

Leave ¼"   Leave ¼"

Center (wrong side)   Border unit made with 3 fabric strip (right side)

45°

2. To attach the border to the center section of the quilt, center each border on a side so the ends extend equally on either side of the center section. Beginning and ending with a backtack, sew the border to the center with a ¼" seam; sew from seam line to seam line, leaving ¼" unsewn at the beginning and end. Press seam allowances toward the border.

3. Arrange the first corner to be mitered on the ironing board, as illustrated. Align the edges of the borders, pinning the center pieced

section out of the way. Press the borders flat and straight. Pin the quilt to the ironing board to keep it from slipping.

Using the Bias Square™, a 90°/45° triangle, or other ruler with a 45° angle marking, draw a line that begins at the inside seam allowance, where the previous stitches stopped, and lies at a 45° angle to the outside edge of the borders. This is the sewing line. Pin in place.

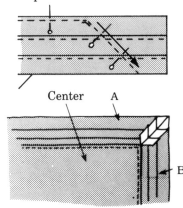

Center   A

B

4. Backtacking at the beginning, stitch on the drawn line from the inside ¼" seam line to outside edge. Trim excess fabric to ¼" along the mitered seam. Press mitered seam open. Press other seams to the outside.

Preparing to Quilt

MARKING

In most cases, the quilt top must be marked with lines to guide stitching, before you quilt. Where you place the quilting lines will depend on the patchwork design, the type of batting used, and how much quilting you want to do.

Try to avoid quilting too close to the seam lines, where the bulk of seam allowances might slow you down or make the stitches uneven. Also, keep in mind that the purpose of quilting, besides its aesthetic value, is to securely hold the three layers together. Don't leave large areas unquilted.

Thoroughly press the quilt top and mark it, before it is assembled with the batting and backing. You will need marking pencils; a long ruler or yardstick; stencils or templates for quilting motifs; and a smooth, clean, hard surface on which to work. Use a sharp marking pencil and lightly mark the quilting lines on the fabric. No matter what kind of marking tool you use, light lines will be easier to remove than heavy ones.

BACKING

You often can use a single length of 45" wide fabric for backing small quilts. To be safe, plan on a usable width of only 42" after shrinkage and cutting of selvages. For larger quilts, you will have to sew two lengths of fabric together.

Cut the backing 1" larger than the quilt top, all the way around. Press thoroughly with seams open.

BATTING

Batting is the filler in a quilt or comforter. Thick batting is used in comforters that are tied. If you plan to quilt, use thin batting and quilt by hand.

Thin batting comes in 100% polyester, 100% cotton, and a cotton-polyester (80%-20%) combination. All-cotton batting requires close quilting to prevent shifting and separating in the wash. Most old quilts have cotton batting and are rather flat. Cotton is a good natural fiber that lasts well and is compatible with cotton and cotton-blend fabrics.

Less quilting is required on 100% polyester batting. If polyester batting is glazed or bonded, it is easy to work with, won't pull apart, and has more loft than cotton. Some polyester batting, however, has a tendency to "beard" or "migrate" (the small white polyester fibers creep to the quilt's surface between the threads in the fabric). This migration most often occurs when polyester blends are used in the quilt top instead of 100% cotton fabrics. The cotton-polyester batting is said to combine the best features of the two fibers. You also can use a single layer of preshrunk cotton flannel for filler instead of batting. The quilt will be very flat, and quilting stitches highly visible.

ASSEMBLING THE LAYERS

Lay the backing face down on a large, clean, flat surface. With masking tape, tape the backing down (without stretching) to keep it smooth and flat while you are working with the other layers.

Gently lay the batting on top of the backing, centering and smoothing it as you go. It is a good idea to let the batt "relax" for a few hours at this point, to ease out wrinkles. Trim batting to size of backing.

Center the freshly ironed and marked quilt top on top of the batting, right side up. Starting in the middle, pin baste the three layers together while gently smoothing out fullness to the sides and corners. Take care not to distort the straight lines of the quilt design and the borders.

After pinning, baste the layers together with needle and light-colored thread. Start in the middle and make a line of long stitches to each corner to form a large X. Continue basting in a grid of parallel lines 6"–8" apart. Finish with a row of basting around the outside edges. Quilts that are to be quilted with a hoop or on your lap will be handled more than those quilted on a frame; therefore, they will require more basting.

After basting, remove the pins. Now you are ready to quilt.

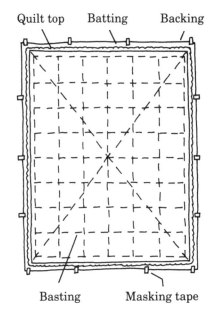

Quilt top   Batting   Backing

Basting   Masking tape

Hand Quilting

To quilt by hand, you will need quilting thread, quilting needles, small scissors, a thimble, and perhaps a balloon or large rubber band to help grasp the needle if it gets stuck. Quilt on a frame, a large hoop, or just on your lap or a table. Use a single strand of quilting thread not longer than 18". Make a small single knot in the end of the thread. The quilting stitch is a small running stitch that goes through all three layers of the quilt. Take two, three, or even four stitches at a time if you can keep them even. When crossing seams, you might find it necessary to "hunt and peck" one stitch at a time.

To begin, insert the needle in the top layer about ³/₄" from the point you want to start stitching. Pull the needle out at the starting point and gently tug at the knot until it pops through the fabric and is buried in the batting. Make a backstitch and begin quilting. Stitches should be tiny (8–10 per inch is good), even, and straight. At first, concentrate on even and straight; tiny will come with practice.

When you come almost to the end of the thread, make a single knot ¼" from the fabric. Take a backstitch to bury the knot in the batting. Run the thread off through the batting and out the quilt top; snip it off. The first and last stitches will look different from the running stitches in between. To make them less noticeable, start and stop where quilting lines cross each other or at seam joints.

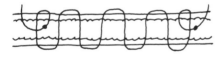

Hand quilting stitch

Binding

BIAS STRIPS

Binding that will be used to finish the edges of a quilt is usually made from bias strips of fabric. To find the true bias, bring one side of fabric to the adjacent side and press, or use a ruler with a 45° angle marking. Using a rotary cutter and mat, cut 1½" wide strips along the bias. One-half yard of fabric will yield 5¼ yards of 1½" bias binding. Three-fourths yard of fabric will yield 12 yards of 1½" bias binding.

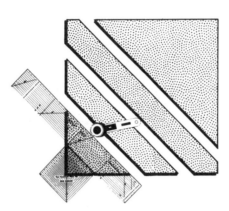

Cutting bias strips

Seam ends together to make a continuous strip long enough to go around your quilt, with a few extra inches for joining.

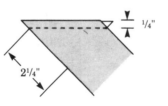

BINDING THE EDGES

After quilting, trim excess batting and backing even with the edge of the quilt top. A rotary cutter and long ruler will ensure accurate straight edges. If basting is no longer in place, baste all three layers together.

1. Using a ¼" seam allowance, sew the binding strips to the front of the quilt. Begin at the center of one side and sew through all layers. Be careful not to stretch the bias or the quilt edge as you sew. Stitch until you reach the seam line point at the corner. Backstitch; cut threads.
2. Turn quilt to prepare for sewing along the next edge. Fold the binding away from the quilt, as shown, then fold again to place binding along edge of quilt. (This fold creates an angled pleat at corner.)

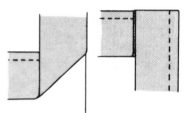

3. Stitch from the fold of the binding along the seam line to the seamline point at the next corner. Backstitch; cut threads. Fold binding as in step 2 and continue around edge.
4. Join the beginning and ending of the binding strip, or plan to hand sew one end to overlap the other.
5. Turn binding to the back side, turning raw edge under, and blindstitch in place. At each corner, fold binding in the sequence shown to form a miter on back of quilt.

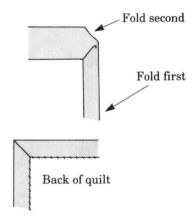

Fold second

Fold first

Back of quilt